An
GHOST
Volume 2

True Encounters
with
Ghosts

Lex Wahl

Preface

Welcome to Volume Two of the Anything Ghost collection of personal ghost stories.

Anything Ghost is a podcast (audio show) where people send their paranormal experiences and I read them on the show (or some people narrate their own stories...in fact, there are a few of those popular stories included in this volume.

Anything Ghost was founded in January of 2006, and was the first podcast to share personal experiences with ghosts—a genre that has since exploded in the podcast world.

To compile this book, I have sifted through countless email, reached out to those who sent in their stories, transcribed self-narrated stories, asked for any photographs they would like to include...and put together this collection of true paranormal experiences. I have made edits to the stories, but what I've included in this book is basically what I read when the story was sent to me. Also, for those who are interested in hearing the original recordings, each story is followed by the show's episode number. The complete archive of Anything Ghost episodes is available to the Anything Ghost VIP "Ghroup" (check out www.anythingghost.com for more information on becoming a member of the VIP Ghroup).

While compiling the book (rummaging through archived email; dusting off old Word documents; sifting through archives of audio of files), I remembered that some people sent photographs along with their stories. So with their approval, I began adding some of those photos to the book—some went back to the place of their experience, and took fresh pictures; and one contributor even created a drawing of his experience (see page 99).

The Anything Ghost Show has always been about the stories—and it wouldn't be "anything" without those who shared their experiences. A heart-felt-thanks goes out to everyone who has shared experiences on Anything Ghost—and a special thanks to those who allowed me to share their experiences and pictures in Anything Ghost Volume 2.

As with Volume 1, my hope is that this book will not only be a great source of ghostly entertainment, but that it can also be used as an insightful look into what may be going on all around us... tap, tap, tap.

Start flipping the pages, and come relive other people's True Encounters with Ghosts!

Take care!
Lex

Table of Contents

Chapter One

Those gloomy, flour, so dark, so damp, so cold.

Basements and Attics

All houses wherein men have lived and died
Are haunted houses. Through the open doors
The harmless phantoms on their errands glide,
With feet that make no sound upon the floors.

We meet them at the door-way, on the stair,
Along the passages they come and go,
Impalpable impressions on the air,
A sense of something moving to and fro.

(Poem Continues in Chapter 2)

The Basement at Grandma's House
Matt (Sudbury, Ontario, Canada)

I grew up in the same small town as my grandparents; so needless-to-say, we spent a lot of time at their house—whenever we had a family dinner or celebration, it was at their house. They built the house in 1962, and my dad and all of his siblings grew up there.

My grandma swore that house was haunted. But she believed the presence was not malevolent, and that it was merely deceased family members watching over us.

There was nothing ghostly in the house until 1989: that's when my great grandmother passed away. She didn't die in the house, but she had lived there for many years with my grandma. My grandma said that after my great grandmother passed away, she felt her presence in the house. Sometimes, my grandma could distinctly smell her perfume.

My oldest personal memory of a ghostly encounter in the house was when I was around eight or ten years old. The basement of the house had a rec room with wood paneling, and shag carpeting. My uncle (who was special needs), lived there with my grandparents. He had an old Nintendo in the basement that my sister and I played Super Mario on. Next to the TV hung a large, antique portrait of my great grandfather in his WWI uniform.

One afternoon, I was playing Nintendo down there, and I heard a monotone moan come from what seemed to be right behind the TV. I was immediately freaked out and ran up the stairs and out of the basement. It took me a few years to be able to go back down there alone. I don't know if it actually was my great grandfather—but the proximity of the portrait to where I heard the moan was enough to spook me.

Unfortunately, in 2009, my grandmother passed away. Ever since my great grandma passed away, my grandma wanted to make sure that we knew when she passed away: she told us that she would flicker lights to let us know she was there. Sure enough, shortly after we held her funeral, the bathroom lights at my own house flickered while on. It was comforting to know she was still around. Since then, there have been a few occasions she has flickered the lights to let me know she was watching over me—most notably after I started a new job.

In 2010, my uncle (who had lived with my grandparents) passed away; and then in 2015 my grandpa had to move to a nursing home. At that point, we began the process of cleaning out the house so it could to be sold.

"They built the house in 1962..."

Once again, I found myself alone in the rec room in the basement—this time on the other side of the room (behind the bar counter). I was moving things out of the shelves, when a strong, distinct whisper floated next to my left ear—as if someone was whispering directly in my ear while floating by. Again spooked, I left the basement until I could go down there with someone else. That was spookier to me than the moaning I heard as a kid, as this time I distinctly felt the whispering go by. I told my family about it, but I was never taken seriously.

Shortly after that, the house was sold and we had to say goodbye forever. I don't know the new owners, so I cannot say whether they have had experiences. However, I would like to hope that my family members who were watching over us, have moved on.

Earlier this year, my grandpa passed away. He was a rather serious person, and to my knowledge he never thought about ghosts. Not long after he passed away, the treadmill that we had in our basement, turned on by itself and sped up to full speed. I don't know if it was related to my grandpa passing away (if it was him saying hello), but it was a scary experience.

Anything Ghost Show, Episode #225

Growing Up Ghostly
Katerina (Ottawa, Ontario, Canada)

We lived in a raised bungalow. The area that would be considered the basement was fully renovated into another living space: kitchen, living room, bedroom, and bathroom. Living there at the time were my grandmother, my mother and father, and myself. My grandmother had the basement, and my parents and I had the main level of the home.

Growing up there, I would sometimes sleep walk, have night terrors, and see shadow figures. Occasionally, as I stood in the living room and looked down the hallway (which, because there were no windows, was dark even during the day if there were no lights on), I would often see a tall, lanky shadow figure slide from my bedroom into my parents' bedroom.

At one point, my night terrors got so bad that my mother piled blankets at the foot of her bed for me to sleep on: because I would call and call for them to stay in my room while I slept (I was getting to be too big to sleep between them, but I didn't mind sleeping at the foot of their bed).

At that time, my parents would leave the bedroom doors open because our two cats would cycle between sleeping in their room and the living room. I remember waking up one night, sleeping on the pile of blankets, and looking across the hall into my bedroom. I had a clear visual shot of the chair in my room, where my dad would often sit while waiting for me to fall asleep. Sitting in that chair was a dark mass—of which I could only make out a head and shoulders. I threw the covers over my head, and remained that way until I eventually fell asleep.

I eventually ended up sleeping downstairs with my grandmother; that was the only place I didn't see the shadow figure. But even while with my grandmother, if I woke up late at night, I would hear footsteps pacing around on the main level above. One morning, I asked my mum why her or dad was awake at 3 AM pacing around; she told me neither of them had been pacing around.

Fast-forward a few years. We moved into a new house in Ottawa, Ontario. I was fifteen, and I was thrilled to leave that other house. By that age, I had taken an interest in horror movies: I felt less alone knowing that what I was experiencing was real enough to be turned into TV shows and movies. But the new house was no better than the last—and to this day, I don't do well there.

My parents never experienced anything in the old house, and they still don't understand what I'm so afraid of at the current house in Ottawa. However, my friends that would stay over during our high school years, and even now, tell me stories of seeing a shadow figure move around the house.

One of the scariest situations I've ever experienced in that house was only a few months ago.

On the second floor, my bedroom and the guest room are across from each other. One night, for a change of scenery, I decided to sleep in the guest room. My bedroom was set up so my bed was pushed against the wall (opposite of the door). When my door was open, I could see across the hall and into the guest room. I had the exact same view of my bedroom when I lied in the guest bed.

It was fairly early into the night as I began to crawl into bed, but I began to feel extremely uneasy: as if being in the guest bed was the worst thing I could be doing—like I was crossing some imaginary boundary line. Trying to ignore it, I snuggled into the blankets. That's when I looked into my unlit bedroom. In the bed in that room, I saw a person facing away from me—more specifically, a girl. I could make out very clearly, long black hair spread across the pillow and shoulders under the blankets. The blankets were a dark purple, but I could see the difference in texture of the darker hair against the blankets. I began to scream, and I called for my dad! My dad came running up to see me. But when I got him to look in my room, my bed was completely flat and the blankets untouched—no shape of a girl sleeping on her side.

"But the new house was no better than the last..."

Since that night, I sleep in my own bed, with the door closed, and I burn sage every night before bed.

I could talk for days about the things I experienced on a weekly basis, but I'll tell you one more brief experience.

I've been with my current boyfriend for three years, and he's been around our house for quite some time—even before we started dating. He's grown up with ghostly, unexplained experiences, so he's pretty good at handling the things he experiences in my house.

Our main level has a few rooms off the hallway and entrance, but once it opens up into the kitchen, the sunroom and dining room are side by side in an open concept style. Gavin and I were sitting in the sunroom, and from there we had a clear view of the dining room, kitchen, and the hallway to the front door (which was where my dad's office and the study branch off).

"I saw someone walk from the study and across the hallway..."

It was just before 6 PM, and Gavin and I were chatting. My mom was in the kitchen prepping food, and my dad was standing and talking to her. Suddenly, Gavin stopped his story, and asked me, "Who else is here?"

Confused, I shook my head and said, "What do you mean?"

He shrugged, "Nah, it's nothing. Don't worry. I don't want to spook you."

Since the girl in my bed incident, I prefer not to discuss whatever we see in the house, because I don't want to give it power.

But being stubborn, I told him I wanted to know.

He replied, "I saw someone walk from the study, across the hallway, and into your dad's office."

At night, when you're alone, the house takes on a weird feeling. You feel the need to run up the stairs—you don't want to leave the lights off, and any noise makes you jump. The lights often flicker and dim (despite my dad constantly checking the electricity). It's not an old home, it's probably about ten-years-old—which makes me wonder if whatever was with me in the previous home, followed us four hours to Ottawa.

I also find it unusual that my parents and my grandmother never experienced anything in Toronto—and my parents still have yet to experience or see what I do in our home in Ottawa. But my friends can vouch (and so can my boyfriend Gavin). I smudge my room every night, while mentally asking whatever force is with us, to leave my family and me alone.

I also would like to note that I still get really bad night terrors, and sleep tests are unable to figure out why.

Anything Ghost Show, Episode #244

Brother's Future Doppelgänger
Antonio (Rhode Island, U.S.)

I'm the younger of two kids. My mom got pregnant with my older brother fairly early in her married life. My father was, well, doing other things, so my mom was usually left to do everything around the house.

She lived in a house that included a basement that had many stories of its own—one of those stories was an incident where my ex-wife was doing laundry, and the basement suddenly became cold; at that instant, she felt something breathing behind her; then she heard a deep growl—as if to warn her to get out. Needless-to-say, she bolted up the stairs, and told me all about it

Another story regarding the basement: we decided to see if we could capture any electronic voice phenomena (EVP). We made sure it was a time where it was only us alone in the house, and we set a tape recorder on the basement stairs; we then left the room, locking the door behind us. The door was hard to open and even banging around the door won't unlock it. We went to retrieve the recorder, and noted that the door was still locked. Nobody had come in or out of the house. Upon reviewing the audio, we heard the basement door open and footsteps slowly going down the stairs. That was followed by the sound of footsteps going back up the stairs, and the door closing again. As I said, we were alone the whole time. We also heard what sounded like a little girl say, "Daddy, daddy." This freaked us out as we have kids of our own—But our children where at school. I again heard this little girl a few months later as I was drifting off to sleep. I heard her say, "Daddy, daddy." I woke up thinking one of my daughters was home. But it was an empty house, and I was left questioning what was going on.

The layout of the house was: the basement, then first floor, then second floor, then a dinky stair case the led to our attic. Our attic had two rooms, so it was used mostly for storage.

One time, my mother was in the attic putting stuff away. Something drew her attention to a mirror on the door, and that's when she saw a man. He had a dark beard and dark hair; his eyes where green and he had a slightly tan complexion. My mother said he didn't seem evil or mad—more curious than anything. Of course, she didn't really like this so she quickly ran down the stairs.

Soon after that incident, my brother was born, and years later I came along; we were both healthy babies. I had a twin who was born with me, but unfortunately he did not survive birth. My mother later told me that she believes the man she saw in the mirrors years ago, looked exactly how my brother now looks in his twenties: beard, hair, green eyes and all.

I wonder if this was a premonition or perhaps a doppelgänger who showed itself to my mother? Or maybe it changed itself to make my brother look like it? I often wonder what it wanted. Does my brother look like someone who has since long passed? Or has a spirit taken over his body to be reborn and enjoy a new life?

Anything Ghost Show, Episode #224

Visits from a Ghost Girl
Paula (U.S.)

In the late 1980's, my husband and I were newly married and living in a townhouse we had recently purchased. The house was part of a development built on farmland that had been in the same family since the 18th century. The original farmhouse remained on the property with the descendants of the family still living in the home.

We had been living in our house for several months, when every night I began to wake up at around 3 AM. One night in particular, I was up and staring straight ahead. I saw the figure of a girl who appeared to be about ten-years-old with long blond hair. She was dressed in an old-fashioned country type dress, and looked disheveled and dirty (as though she had been playing in the dirt). She was gliding straight toward the bed. By the time she arrived at the center of the foot of the bed, I was terrified; she then went to what would be her left, and headed toward the side of the bed where my husband was sleeping. I put my head under the covers in fear and eventually fell asleep.

The next morning, I told my husband what I had seen, and he told me that he had seen the exact same thing. He added that the ghost girl floated at the foot of the bed, and then she turned to go over to his side of the bed. She stood in front of his nightstand looking directly at him and vanished. Unknown to me at the time, he was also waking up every night around 3 AM.

A couple weeks after we saw the ghost girl, my husband and I were grocery shopping at a nearby market. We were at the check out counter where the cashier was a teenage girl with long blond hair—who looked exactly like our ghost girl, only older. My husband I looked at each other in shock, and knew we were thinking the same thing: the resemblance this girl had with our ghost girl could not be a coincidence. I gave the teenage cashier a check to pay for the groceries; she looked at the address on the check, and said, "Oh! You live on what was my family's farmland."

After the encounter with the teenage cashier, my husband and I believe the ghost girl was a residual type haunting. The little spirit girl had possibly been a family member from the original farm family (due to the uncanny resemblance between our visitor in the night and the member of the original farm family at the market). The ghostly encounter was both amazing and terrifying!

Anything Ghost Show, Episode #240

Chapter Two

Bathrooms

There are more guests at table than the hosts
Invited; the illuminated hall
Is thronged with quiet, inoffensive ghosts,
As silent as the pictures on the wall.

(Poem Continues in Chapter 3)

The Loop
Jae (Florida, U.S.)

This happened to me when I was thirteen years old. At that age, a lot of the time on the weekends, I was at home alone. My younger brother would be staying with a cousin or a friend, and my parents were often at some friends' home (they were very social).

One weekend in particular, I was playing Sega Genesis and I decided after a while to take a shower. I gathered all my shower belongings and headed to the shower room. I was taking a shower, and everything was fine, when suddenly, the shower curtain jerked to the side and opened. At that point, I found myself standing face to face with a stranger. Involuntarily, I jumped back, slipped and fell. In doing so, the back of my head hit the back of the shower and I winced (because it hurt pretty bad). After I recovered, I looked back toward the man... he was gone—not a trace of him in sight.

I froze. But it didn't take long for me to jump out of the shower, run to the bathroom door and lock it. My heart was beating fast; I was shaking and trying to figure out what to do next.

The bathroom door was flimsy and could easily be kicked in, so there wasn't a lot between me and whoever it was I saw. So I figured I had to do something quick—I couldn't just stay in the bathroom, because I didn't know if he was there to rob our home, kill me, or what.

So I quickly got dressed, and decided the best thing to do was to make a bee-line for the front door. It was about twenty feet away from the bathroom—and I was a pretty swift child (as I played sports)—so I was confident I could make it. But it was little risky because we didn't leave a lot of lights on in the house. Without much more thought, I jumped from the bathroom, sprinted to the front door and made it outside.

Once outside, I ran across the street to the neighbor's house, went straight to the door and found my mom. I was bent over, breathing hard, and she was trying to figure out what was wrong with me. After I caught my breath, I explained to her what happened. She immediately jumped up, went to where my father was, and told him what happened. The neighbor heard the story, and grabbed his gun. They then all started walking toward the house. My mom was screaming to my father, asking if she should call the police. My dad said they could handle it.

In about five or ten minutes they returned and said everything was as it should be in the house. Nothing was taken; everything was fine except for the front door being open (that was because I didn't even try to close it on my way out).

After we went home that night, everybody slept in the same room. The last thing I recall was my father sitting in a chair and keeping watch.

Nothing happened after that—I was weirded out for a little while, but everything went back to normal.

A couple years later, I joined the Navy. I did a lot of traveling and then I came back. I was the age of twenty-two, and found a place to live about an hour and a half away from my parents' house.

Being that I lived so close, I made plans to go home for the Fourth of July (U.S. Independence Day). On the Fourth of July, the family all went down to the bay to watch the fireworks. The bay was only about three blocks from my parents' house, so it was a short walk.

However, when I woke up in the morning on the fourth, I didn't feel well. I felt kind of nauseous and I just didn't feel like walking down to the bay to see the fireworks. So I told my mother I was not going to go with them. The family left, and said they would be back shortly.

Now by myself at the house, I thought I would take some Tylenol, watch TV and relax. I decided to first take a shower, so I gathered all my things and proceeded to the bathroom. Once I got to the bathroom, I put everything down, and then pulled back the shower curtain. This was when things got really weird.

After pulling back the shower curtain, I saw my younger self-standing in the shower. We were looking at each other face-to-face. I immediately remembered what had happened that day when I was younger. But I was scared anyways, because my mind just couldn't process or make sense of what was happening. Then I saw my younger self fall and hit his (or my) head on the shower wall.

I started backing up, trying to get away, because I was afraid of what was happening. As I was backing away, I tripped and fell. I rolled over and crawled for the bathroom door, opened it, and crawled out into the hall. I was sitting on my hands and knees, trying to figure out what just happened. I got up, paced around for a little bit, and tried to decide what to do next. I decided I should go back into the bathroom to clear up the mystery. But like a coward, I opened the door slowly and stood against the sidewall. Then I just kind of peaked my head inside of the bathroom. I didn't know what I was going to see at that point. A ghost? An alien?

So after I peaked around the corner, I looked into the shower and nobody was there. I continued into the bathroom to examine the shower, and found that the shower was dry—as if no one had been in there! I distinctly remember seeing my younger self in the shower with the water running. I also recall that at that moment there was no sound when I saw my younger self in the shower.

So I walked back out into the living room, sat down and waited for my parents to come back.

When my parents returned, I explained to them what happened. They looked at me like I was strange.

And then I told them, "Remember when I was young, and I saw that man as I was standing in the shower? Well that man was me! I think I ran into my older self that day!"

My mom started laughing, and asked what it was I was smoking.

But my father suggested, "Maybe you got caught in a time loop."

I don't know if it was a time loop, but that's the story of what happened to me. I've never been able to find any explanation for what happened to me on those two days of my life.

Anything Ghost Show, Episode #231

The Poltergeist on Cartwright Street
Andy (Toronto, Ontario)

Back in 2000 to 2003, my friend lived in a little apartment in the upstairs of a house while he was going to University in London, Ontario. The apartment was quite small, it had a small living room, a tiny bathroom, a tiny kitchen and a tiny bedroom—needless to say it was pretty tiny. But we'd get a dozen people in there at a time, and because of the proximity of the house to the downtown, it was a central 'hang-out' spot for a lot of our friends.

One night there were a few of us hanging out watching TV, when all of a sudden, the tap in the bathroom turned on. I asked my friend whose apartment it was, why his tap just turned on by itself.

He told me it happens all the time, and just assumed it was something to do with the plumbing. My friend got up and turned the tap off.

One of the next times it happened, as soon as the tap went on, I rushed to the bathroom to see for myself. It was an old sink with a separate HOT and COLD faucet. The hot faucet was turned all the way on, blasting steaming hot water, so I turned it off—it took 2-3 full turns shut off. The strangest part about it was that because it was in the upstairs of an older house, it usually took a fair amount of time for the water to get hot—but when it turned on by itself, it would be steaming hot (not to mention, the handle would have to be rotated several times to turn on full blast).

This went on for years after the incident that I witnessed; it would turn on so much that we became desensitized to it.

My friend was a bit of a neat freak, because his apartment was so small; he kept it very tidy, including his tiny kitchen. One evening, a few of us left his place to go to a few bars and meet some friends. At the end of the night I decided to crash on my friend's couch because I was a bit drunk and didn't want to drive home.

When we got up to his apartment, we both went into the kitchen to grab a few beers from the fridge, where we found all his kitchen cupboards open and all the plates, cups, bowls and cutlery, piled and stacked on the counter and in the sink, as if someone was going to wash all the dishes after a big meal. Somehow this had happened while we were out with zero explanation of how it happened. He did say that he'd come home other times and find his cupboards and kitchen a mess like that, too.

Other times he said that he'd come home from school or work and find ALL of his lights on as well, he said that happened a lot, too.

There were also other times that we'd be sitting watching TV and there'd be a knock on his door downstairs. When someone went to go and see who it was, most of the time there'd be nobody there.

I personally was there for many of these incidents and even answered an empty doorway a few times, too. It's especially disappointing when you think it's the pizza guy. This also became so common place that when someone would go down and find and empty doorway they'd yell up, "False alarm guys, its just the ghost."

After University my friend moved out of there and never looked back. But every once in a while, I think about that place and have always been curious to knock on the door and ask the new occupants if they've experienced the same thing—maybe I will some day.

Anything Ghost Show, Episode #241

Chapter Three

Bedrooms

The stranger at my fireside cannot see
The forms I see, nor hear the sounds I hear;
He but perceives what is; while unto me
All that has been is visible and clear.

(Poem Continues in Chapter 4.)

The Man in the Corner

Ivy (U.S.)

At the time of this story, I was about nine, so it was about four years ago.

I was trying going to sleep (it was late, around 1:00 AM), and other than a night-light, it was completely dark in my room (the night-light didn't really make a difference in the darkness of my room). I was about to doze off when I was filled with the feeling of being watched—but I didn't feel like I was in trouble or like something was coming to hurt me. I had my own room, and I had not heard the door open, so I knew it wasn't my brother or mom.

I opened my eyes and scanned around my room; it seemed like there was nothing with me, until I looked at the corner of the room—right next the door. Standing there was a figure; a tall figure (maybe around six feet). It was darker than the room itself—it was a huge dark shadow. It looked as if it was staring at me, even though I could see no eyes. I stared back at it. My eyes often play tricks on me, so my first thought was that it was just my imagination

But then, it started to move. It didn't walk: it was more like it was at one spot and then suddenly it was closer.

I started to get freaked out, but I didn't move. I was sleeping in the top portion of a bunk bed, so when this man got close enough, his face was inches away from my face.

I finally got scared enough to move. I sat up and quickly turned on my lamp. It was gone.

I turned off my lamp again to see if it was still there (and was perhaps just part of my imagination), but it was gone.

I then ran into my mom's room and slept in her bed that night—and for a few nights after that.

Luckily, she and most of the people I told about this story to, believed me.

I never got that feeling, or saw that man, ever again.

Anything Ghost Show, Episode #224

Whispers in the Night

Josie (Texas, U.S.)

Back when I was married, we were living in a house out in the open country with very few houses near by. The house always had a cold feeling: it felt as though we were always being watched. Shadows would dart from room to room; we'd hear sounds like something was moving; or the sounds of doors closing.

Even today, the house stands vacant.

I had several experiences there, but the one that I'm going to tell happened when my then husband was there.

It was close to midnight and we were getting ready for bed; the lights had been turned off, as well as the TV, and cell phones had been silenced for the night. My then husband was already in bed and I had just lifted up the blankets on my side, when we heard some voices near the front door. Our bedroom was not that far from the front door (and the house was quiet), so we were able to hear the voices.

We had a surveillance system, and we both looked at the screen to see if we could see who was at our door. Since his mom lived next door we assumed it was her and a man, but when we looked at the screen there was no one at our front door. We scanned all the other cameras that faced the front yard but we couldn't see anyone out there.

Through all of this we kept quiet and we could still hear the voices. Then suddenly, the voices sounded as if they were in our sitting room; and just as suddenly these voices moved through our dining room; then to our kitchen; then through our bedroom; and finally out of the door that led onto our patio.

Just as quickly as they moved through our house and exited, we couldn't hear them anymore.

We weren't able to make out what they were saying, but it was clearly the voice of a woman and a man.

Anything Ghost Show, Episode #224

Goodbye, Old Friend
Brandi (Texas, U.S.)

When I was a little girl my mom was part of a bowling league. Every week she would get together with her team and I would go with her to get out of the house for a little while. She stuck with this for years, and her teammates eventually became like extended family. One member in particular was like a big brother to her, and like an uncle to me.

They were extremely close, so when we found out he had cancer we were devastated. Not too long after his diagnosis, he passed away. The night we found out he died, I decided to sleep in my mom's room so she wouldn't be alone.

I remember waking up in the middle of the night and looking near my mom—I couldn't believe my eyes. Sitting beside my mom was a dark shadowy figure. The figure had no distinct features, but I could see the outline of a cap and glasses; I knew without a doubt it was him, since that was always what he wore. I pulled the covers all the way up to my neck and tried my hardest not to breathe too loudly. I kept watching, and then the thought crossed my mind, "You're not supposed to be here."

The figure whipped its head around in my direction, as if it read my mind, and I threw the cover over my head.

My heart was pounding so hard that I thought it would explode. After a few tense seconds, I moved the cover away to see if he was still there, but he was gone.

I told my mom the next day, but I'm not sure if she believed me or not. She just smiled as if to pacify me; but I know what I saw: and that has stuck with me all these years.

I just think it was nice of him to come and say goodbye.

Anything Ghost Show, Episode #225

The Hatman in My Bedroom

Zoe (Kansas City, Kansas)

I've always been at least kind of aware of ghosts, even if it's just a vague tingling down my back or a shape on the edge of my periphery (I sometimes half-joke that I must be haunted, since things always seem to find their way to me). For the most part they don't worry me much at all, with one main exception. When I was growing up, I went between my mom's house during the week and my dad's house on the weekend. Which was fine, I liked getting to relax at my dad's house after my homework was done. However, one place in our small one-story house was far from relaxing. Unfortunately, that one place was my bedroom.

Anytime I went into my room after dark, it felt like someone was watching me—even if the shades were totally drawn. Our lot backed onto a parking lot and the house next to ours sat farther up the street, so all I could see out my side window was their small back porch. There was no way anyone could have been watching me without me seeing them.

This feeling of being watched didn't change from day-to-day: if I was in my room after dark, I felt cold and anxious, but not during the day. It got to the point to where I refused to sleep in my room (preferring instead to sleep on the couch, or in my dad's bed—if he fell asleep in my living room).

When I was ten, my dad's girlfriend moved in and started insisting that I sleep in my own room. Very reluctantly, I went to sleep in my own room—but only if she or my dad went across the room to turn on the paper lantern that hung over my bed (which served as my only artificial light source in the room). Because I would always read before bed, I used to leave the light on when I fell asleep: if the light was on, I wasn't scared.

A few times I would wake up in the middle of the night and the light would be off (probably my dad or his girlfriend had come in and turned it off before they went to bed). These were always my least favorite nights. I would hide under the blankets and quilts that layered my bed (regardless of the heat), in that childish conviction that if I was hidden, whatever it was couldn't get to me.

One night, I woke up with the light off and failed to hide quickly enough. I was lying on my side, facing the window and suddenly the window I was looking at seemed like it was getting darker (while the other windows stayed the same). Eventually, the darkness condensed into the shape of a man in a tall hat. I couldn't see the details of his face, except for bright red eyes. I could blink but struggled to get control of my arms to duck under my blankets for a little while. Finally, I was able to hide and I slowly felt the fear that had overwhelmed me dissipate.

In the morning I tried to explain what had happened to my dad and his girlfriend, and why I didn't want to sleep in my room anymore. They said it was probably just a dream. I didn't think so, but I didn't argue and kept sleeping in my room—always making sure the light was on when I went to sleep. After my dad's girlfriend moved out, I was able to go back to sleeping in the living room or in dad's bedroom.

A number of years later (after I had stopped spending as much time at my dad's house), I was talking about the incident with a few of my friends, and they told me I should look up, "the Hatman" next time I was online.

Next time I was at the computer I looked it up and found a bunch of stories so similar to mine it gave me chills. They all seemed to happen when the tellers were children—like I was when I saw him.

I've seen and heard other entities or spirits before and since my experience with the Hatman, but none have had the same kind of lead-up or have made me feel the same paralyzing fear the Hatman did.

My dad moved out of that house my senior year of high school, after my grandpa (his dad) died. The house and land was later bought by KU Med Center, the big hospital in Kansas City, Kansas, and the house was torn down.

I live in Kansas City now, after graduating from college in Iowa last year. A couple of times, I have gone back to where the house used to be, and to where my bedroom was—and even in broad daylight, as I was standing there, it still gave me a decidedly unpleasant chill down my spine. It makes me wonder if somehow the Hatman is still there; tied to the ground where the house once stood, and still staring at me.

Anything Ghost Show, Episode #225

Buffy's Ghost Experience
Jennifer (Ottawa, Ontario)

These events happened to my mother when I was about five years old. We had just moved into a house for about three or four months, when the following incidents began to happen.

My mother was asleep in the master bedroom, and woke up in the middle of the night; upon waking up, she saw the figure of a man standing at the foot of her bed. He was slim and very tall (about six or seven feet). The only part of his body that she could not make out was his face—but she could tell it was a male presence.

She did not feel scared, because she sensed this man was very gentle, and non-threatening. He seemed somehow lost; but also curious about her. She had the feeling that he had not died a natural death, but had been murdered. In fact, he seemed to be looking for something.

Jennifer with her brothers and sister in front of the home.

My father was in the bed next to her but was sound asleep and never sensed the presence. This happened seven or eight times, and the first few times she thought she must have been imagining it.

When it first started, the spirit would appear at the foot of the bed; but with each appearance he came closer—and eventually, he was right next to her. That was when she realized it was not going to stop; so she had to do something about the ghost.

My mother consulted a priest at our church, and he told her that the official opinion of the church was that saying a mass in the house would exorcise the spirit (or put it to rest). He came to our house to say the mass. She was never again bothered by the spirit after that.

My mother never told us about the ghost until we were all adults—a long time after we moved away from the house. It was very recently (many decades after these events), that my mother received confirmation there was a death that occurred in our house. She learned this from a neighbour who was a long time resident of the neighbourhood. A nineteen-year-old man had been violently murdered in the very room in which my parents slept. When the murder occurred it was kept very quiet, and was not advertised to newcomers; so she had no way of knowing of the event.

Anything Ghost Show, Episode #229

The Pacing Ghost
Jenny (Los Angeles, California)

When I was in the 7th grade (around 1986), I spent the night at my friend Megan's house. Her family lived in a split-level ranch home that was in a newer residential development far out in the country. This was in the Midwest, in Illinois close to the Iowa border.

Megan and I were close friends at the time and could spend hours talking and laughing about anything and everything. She had a very sarcastic sense of humor, and nothing seemed to impress her.

We took a long walk out in the country, along the winding roads, that went late into the night in the immense quiet and dark. There were no other people around. And I'm sure we talked about ghosts, or the local stories of a lurker in the cornfield watching the kids on the school playground (a story that, as a child, I thought was just made-up by other students; but as an adult I found it was true). Anyway…we finally went back to her house, and I don't remember much more about that evening, until the sounds that woke me from my sleep.

Megan had only a twin bed in her room, and she insisted I sleep on the bed, and she would sleep on the floor (next to me, on my left). I remember she didn't mind sleeping on the floor, and was proud of toughing it out. The head of the bed was directly under a window. And like I said, the house was a split-level ranch, and the window to her bedroom faced the front of the house. It was at the point where the grade slopes away, so the distance out the window to the ground below was probably about fifteen feet.

I woke up slightly around 1:30 AM. I wasn't fully awake, but I could hear something outside the window making noises that sounded like a gravel bed (for landscaping) below. I didn't even know if there was a gravel bed below the window, but from the noise I was hearing it sounded like there was. It sounded like something was in it, but I didn't really think anything of it. We were out in the country, so I imagined a deer walking around making the noise. I just tried to go back to sleep.

The noise didn't stop.

If it was an animal, it would eventually go away; but this was going on for a long time—and there was something else about it that seemed odd.

I started to notice it wasn't the erratic skittering sound an animal would make when digging or rummaging. I listened to it more closely, as I lie in the dark. I became wider and wider awake as I recognized the sound: these were the sounds of footsteps of a person—not an animal. More specifically, it sounded like the slow, deliberate pacing of a man wearing dress shoes, walking across gravel: heel, toe, heel, toe. Stop. Pivot. Heel, toe, heel, toe...

I was now wide awake in the dark. I listened closely, but I didn't have to strain to hear it: the sound was perfectly clear. I could hear the heel of the shoe crunch into the gravel; that was followed by the flat footfall; then the next step, and the next. Stop. Then the distinctive sound of turning around in place, and walking the other direction. It was slowly, repeatedly, pacing back and forth.

I broke out in a cold sweat. I became absolutely terrified. Megan was sound asleep on the floor next to me, but I felt like I was million miles away from her up on the bed, and directly under the window (that was only covered by a sheer curtain).

I was paralyzed with fear—afraid to move a muscle. The sound was right under the window, and I was sure if I looked, I'd see whatever it was. I was both dying to look out the window and absolutely too petrified to do it. I tried to wake up Megan.

"Megan?" I whispered in the dark. "MEGAN?!"

"Hm. What?"

"Do you hear that?"

The pacing hadn't stopped, so we both listened.

"Yeah, I hear it."

"What IS that??" I whispered loudly.

Megan wasn't bothered, but then again, she'd shrug her shoulders at an approaching tornado.

"I dunno." She mumbled.

"It sounds like someone walking back and forth!" I said.

She sat up and listened for a bit.

"Yeah, it does. Weird. I'm going back to sleep."

I remember being annoyed that she didn't think anything of it—even though she agreed it sounded just like a person walking outside.

"Megan? Will you look out the window?"

"No way. I'm not looking out there."

I was SO frustrated with her! How could she hear it, agree what it was, and just want to go back to sleep? I couldn't. I HAD to look out the window, even though I was absolutely terrified to do so. This wasn't nothing: this sound was really happening.

"I'm going to look out the window. But I want you awake while I do!"

Megan sighed.

One of the most terrifying things I've ever done in my life was to sit up, turn around, lift up that curtain, and press my nose to the window for a look.

The sound stopped.

I saw nothing.

I couldn't see to the ground below; I couldn't see any gravel bed; I could barely see the end of the driveway—which was too far for the sound to be coming from anyway...and there was nothing there.

I couldn't hear the sound any more.

I laid back down; confused by seeing nothing—and having heard something so distinct.

Then...the pacing started back up again.

Megan was already back asleep.

I broke out in a cold sweat.

The sound continued in exactly the same way—pacing across gravel for HOURS. All I could do was to lie wide awake in the dark; scared out of my mind; until sleep took over around 5 AM.

The next morning, I asked Megan about it.

But all she would muster was, "Yeah, that was weird."

I was exhausted from being awake and terrified all night—by what sounded exactly like a man pacing back and forth under the window.

As I left that morning, I took a look at the front of the house, and there were no gravel beds anywhere.

To this day, I have no idea what I was listening to. But the sound was so clear, so distinct, so recognizable, that I know SOMETHING was outside the window that night...but I'll never know what.

Anything Ghost Show, Episode #240

Chapter Four

Cemeteries

We have no title-deeds to house or lands;
Owners and occupants of earlier dates
From graves forgotten stretch their dusty hands,
And hold in mortmain still their old estates.

(Poem Continues in Chapter 5)

Graveside Ghost
Jay (Malta)

My name is Jay and I live on a small island nation called Malta. What Malta lacks in size, it sure makes up in character. Malta's long and winding history, its culture and diverse people make the island a great place to live. The weather is fine and the food is wholesome, and religion, (the Roman Catholic Church) is part of the fabric of this country's rich character.

This story is from my childhood and is my first encounter with the paranormal. When I was seven or eight years old, I joined the parish's altar boys at the local church. My mum, a devout Catholic, encouraged me to serve; and being able to join other children my age and be part of the celebration of mass, interested me a lot. It was a pleasant place for me to go, and after evening mass I was able to hang out with children my age at the adjoining youth centre (where we played table tennis or pool, watched movies or took turns on a PlayStation).

As part of our duties at the church, we served different masses: sometimes there would be a Christening or a wedding; we served Christmas Eve mass or Easter Sunday; but sometimes we also had to serve at funerals. This wasn't a particularly popular mass, and quite often only one or two boys would join the priest for the ceremony. I wasn't really interested in that type of event at first. However, one early morning, I got to the church to find that the morning's mass was a funeral ceremony. I decided to put on my Cassock and Cotta over my clothes and prepare for mass as usual. After all, this is what my duty was anyway. As solemn an occasion it was, I felt good about being able to help, and in a sense, I felt more needed in a funeral than any other type of celebration because not many other altar boys attended funerals. Part of our duty during this ceremony was to complete the occasion with a procession to the cemetery and witness the burial whilst the priest concludes prayer and offers consolation to the mourning congregation. After serving the first funeral, I realized that it was for me and requested to be given the duty of serving future funerals. It wasn't that I relished the occasion or enjoyed the spookiness of it, but I truly felt that it was something good and helpful to the community I was part of.

It was during one such funeral that this encounter with the dead took place. I know the setup was not ideal for an unbiased approach (being that it was an autumn morning at the island's largest cemetery), but later experiences confirmed that what I had been through was as mysterious and spooky, as it was real.

Anna's funeral took place early in the morning. The cold air that filled my lungs as we approached the plot where she was to be laid to rest, complimented the atmosphere quite appropriately.

The few relatives that were at the plot were a quiet bunch—and quite like many other families that lost an old aunt or a grandmother. From my experiences in these occasions, I knew just by looking at the people if the deceased had been sudden or expected; whether the loved one was indeed loved or not; how wealthy the family was, and so on.

Anna's passing was indeed expected. Everyone there seemed to love her enough: with two young twin girls at the front of the small crowd crying as the carriers lowered the coffin to a short pair of stands, before finally lowering the coffin into the ground. The family had requested the coffin be left opened, so they could pay their respects for the final time; and naturally the crying from the young girls intensified as the body's somber face became visible that one last time. Open casket situations are intriguing. Although, whether it was due to fear or respect, I always lowered my eyes and avoided looking at the dead body.

The cold air seemed to grow colder still; and as I stood looking downwards, I began to consciously breathe in and out...watching the exhaling steam wither into the crisp air. I followed a small cloud of steam upwards, and for the first time I noticed a person in the crowd I had not seen before.

She was an old lady—too old looking to be walking upright amongst the bereaved. As she slid through Anna's mourners, I noticed her bare feet: blue and purple veins laced the pair of old gray feet—surely aggravated by the cold morning air! She was making her way to the coffin, and I was sure she was looking at the body (in a sort of half smiling "knowing" sort of a way).

I then realized that it was not the casket she was heading for. She stopped at the girls. Oblivious to everything else, she put her arms around them both; lowered her head, and whispered something into the twins' ears. This appeared to immediately soothe the young sisters.

The moment did not last very long. The old lady lifted her way through the crowd, as if she was sliding through gracefully—making her way to the gaze, and met mine. I recognized the face straight away and smiled back to her as she looked at me (or looked through me), as she squeezed the youngsters' shoulders. Just as sudden as she joined the crowd, she slid right back from where it was she came from, and I lost sight of her.

Confused, I turned immediately to the coffin (that was now being closed), and was able to see the same old lady in her final resting vessel, just before the lid cast a dark shadow over her restful face.

The twins were calm now. Whatever it was they may have heard being whispered into their ears, turned their mood from pure grief to that of an understanding of what is happening...perhaps knowing for the first time that death is not the end.

I continued to see these twins throughout my life, and they recognized me as that young boy who attended their grandma's funeral. Of course, from their demeanor at the time, I was sure they did not see their dear grandma outside the coffin that morning. But I find comfort in knowing that whether they physically felt that embrace, or actually heard those soothing words in their ears, they were able to cope with their loss—and we can, too...with a little help from the memories of those we miss.

Anything Ghost Show, Episode #230

Boy in the Cemetery
Corey (Cincinnati, Ohio)

I'm not exactly a believer in ghosts. I try my best to find rational explanations for everything in life. But when I was a boy, I saw something that all these years later, I still can't find an explanation for.

It happened when I was eleven or twelve. My older brother and I took an overnight trip to a local lake with our church youth group. We spent the night in an old church in a strange little town called Riley, Ohio. In the years since, I've learned that there have been many strange occurrences in Riley. It has a reputation, as it were. There are lots of native burial mounds, old cemeteries, and old houses that look haunted—there were even satanic rituals back in the 70's. It's a weird little place.

The church we stayed in was neat: a small old church, surrounded by cornfields. I believe the church was built in the mid to early 1800's; and right next to the church was a small very old cemetery. Always fascinated with history, I spent most of the evening walking around the graveyard; reading head stones; fascinated by how old they were—while the other kids watched movies inside. I spent all afternoon and evening out there.

As the sun began to set, the church served us dinner. I didn't want to eat inside with everyone else, so I took my food outside. My brother and one of the only boys we liked, joined me.

As we were sitting there eating and joking, we noticed a small boy sitting in the graveyard with his back resting on a head stone. We thought this was odd but we assumed it was a child of one of the church's supervisors. We didn't think "ghost!" or anything. His clothes were outdated, and I knew that even back then: he wore gray wool looking trousers, a white long sleeve button up shirt, suspenders and a matching gray cap. I remember the boy very well. The boy was not paying any attention to us at all. He was just sitting there looking at the ground.

We all decided that it would be funny to sneak up on the boy and scare him. So my brother and I put our friend up to it. We watched as our friend snuck up behind the boy, and then jumped out, shouting. We expected the boy to get very startled (which naturally would have made us all laugh), but he didn't get startled at all. He simply turned his head towards our friend and slowly stood up.

He stood there staring at our friend (our friend staring back at him), in complete silence. Our friend finally—and slowly—started backing away, and then turned and walked very quickly back to my brother and I. All the while, the boy stood staring at him.

Our friend was white as a ghost with a look of panic, so we asked him what happened.

"That kid looks like he's dead. I'm going inside."

My brother and I immediately knew it was a ghost—and we were excited. So we started walking towards the boy—spurred by brotherly emboldening. As we started walking towards the boy, he turned and started walking away. He wasn't far from us, so we started running. He went around the corner and we were only feet behind him; but as we ran around the corner...he was gone.

We quickly ran around the other way and couldn't see him. We looked all over the church (which was very small) and there was no sign of him.

I'm now thirty-two. As the years have gone by, I've tried to chalk this up to anything besides a ghost. But I've never forgotten.

My brother and I didn't speak of it much; I thought he had maybe forgotten. But just a couple of years back, I asked my brother if he remembered that boy in the cemetery?

He very quickly said, "Oh yeah. I remember very well. That was the creepiest thing I've ever seen."

I've recounted my version, and he confirmed every bit.

I've lost touch with the friend who was there with us that night, but I'd love to speak to him and hear his account.

Anything Ghost Show, Episode #228

A Message from the Dead at Mesa Cemetery
Julia (London, UK)

My husband and I were on vacation the past two weeks in Arizona, visiting from the U.K. We were doing all the usual Grand Canyon tourist stuff, and having a great time. One of our loves is aviation history, so we visited the Commemorative Air Force Museum in Mesa. The friendly docent (an elderly guy named Rick, who was a US veteran), explained to us that the museum was built on an old airbase founded by the British Royal Air Force in 1941; and that twenty-three trainee British pilots had died there in air accidents between 1941 and 1944. He also explained that the pilots were all buried together in Mesa Cemetery that was just a few miles down the road.

The next morning we decided to pay our respects at the pilots' graves—seeing as it was close to Veteran's Day, and also the British 'Remembrance Day' (which is commemorated every year on the 11th of November). You should know, that in the UK, most Brits buy a little red paper poppy from the veteran's charity (The Royal British Legion). We pin the poppies to our jackets to show our respect for the fallen. I happened to have my paper poppy with me, and suggested that we leave the poppy there for the British soldiers.

A screenshot of the cryptic message from the cemetery that was left on Julia's locked iPhone.

There were 4 beautiful wreaths at the main memorial stone in front of the twenty-three graves, so I pushed the little plastic stalk of the poppy into the ground in front of them. It looked very pretty there, and we stared at it for a while. After another twenty minutes or so of reading gravestone inscriptions, we both headed out of the cemetery, and found a place to get coffee.

While we were waiting, I got out my iPhone to check my emails; I was shocked to find that, even though my phone had been switched off, there was a note in my message app. It was very weird, because my iPhone can only be activated with a four digit code number, and it turns itself off every five minutes.

In the message I saw the last thing I had typed was a message to my husband: "in lobby." That was just after breakfast. My husband had left the hotel to get gas, and I was waiting for him to come back and pick me up from the lobby. When he did, I jumped in the car and switched off my phone completely.

So we were very shocked (as we waited for our coffee), to see a message in my app that read, "Very pvery, pl phas poppy. Yes."

I think maybe this meant, "Very, very, please, poppy. Yes." Perhaps the "yes" is because I did put the poppy down. It's also weird because there was a full stop (period) before "yes." That's strange because on my phone you have to hold down two keys to do that.

I'm glad that I left the poppy there, because someone definitely wanted it as a reminder of home; but somehow, it was very unnerving.

Anything Ghost Show, Episode #243

Haunt Me If You Can

Steve (Milwaukee, Wisconsin)

When I was seven years old, we lived in an old farmhouse in Wisconsin. The house was next door to an old church cemetery. Though the small country church was long gone, the cemetery was still in use: there were century-old monuments mixed with the more modern, low-to-the ground markers.

Many days I would run around the cemetery with my dog Taffy. I would try to read the worn inscriptions on the oldest tombstones, run around and climb the trees—just generally having a good time for a seven-year-old.

"The house was next door to an old church cemetery..." (photo of Steve's childhood home).

In one corner of the cemetery there was a collection of four rectangular tombstones laid flat on the ground in an open area. While I knew every corner and stone of the place, strangely, I would never play in that corner. I never had any odd feelings or felt any threat, but whenever I intended to go there, something would distract me.

Early one August, I got the crazy idea to go to the cemetery at night—and to try to see a ghost. So one night, after being put to bed, I snuck out of the house and brought our dog Taffy with me. We never kept Taffy on a leash, as she would always stay within about a hundred feet of me no matter where I went. The moonlight was bright enough that night, so I didn't bother bringing a flashlight.

"...I tried stomping on the graves themselves—demanding loudly to be haunted!" (photo of the cemetery)

By that time I was so used to the cemetery that I wasn't afraid at all; to me it was just a neat adventure. After a little thought, I decided the best way to see a ghost was to insult them in some way; so I jumped on a couple of the ground-level tombstones, then waited.

Nothing happened.

The quiet night was only broken by the sounds of crickets, and Taffy sniffing around in some tall grass, looking for mice.

So I tried stomping on the graves themselves—demanding loudly to be haunted!

I waited.

Nothing happened.

Disappointed, I gave up and went home.

Two nights later, I decided to try again. Same as the first night, I snuck out of the house and brought Taffy along. I stomped on some graves, and again demanded to be haunted. Taffy was only a few yards away. What happened next is a bit hard to describe.

I was facing the corner of the cemetery where the four tombstones lay flat on the ground (the corner I never went into). The crickets went silent, and the air above the corner changed—the best I can describe it is that it was like the air froze, then cracked.

Taffy was instantly alert, then immediately bolted away. A fraction of a second later, I followed her—somehow sensing that some kind of "thing" was in the air above chasing after me. I ran faster than I have ever run in my life—I actually beat the Taffy back to the house.

I darted inside and slammed the door behind me. I could sense that the "thing" was now flying around and around the whole outside of the house. There was a terrible panicky growl and scratching at the door—Taffy was still outside! I let her in and she immediately wrapped herself around my legs...shivering.

At that point, my mother was awake and came downstairs wanting to know, "What on earth was going on?!"

She stopped mid-sentence when she saw how terrified Taffy appeared. She knew something was up—which was not surprising since other things had happened in that house. She told me to get back to bed.

By the time I was back in bed, I no longer felt any presence outside at all. I fell asleep quickly.

Needless to say, I never asked to be haunted again.

That is the end of my brother's story. At the time it happened, I was only three years old. But we lived in that house (next to the cemetery) until I was six. There was the time I saw a face looking in a window—a window that was eight feet up. Another time, my brother was in the yard and saw a face looking out from a window in a room we never used. I don't know why our parents never let one of us sleep in that room—we all had to share bedrooms, and that one room was only used for storage.

There was something wrong with that house.

Anything Ghost Show, Episode #244

My Parents Built a House
Nathan (Loxley, Alabama)

Though I now live near the coast of Alabama, every unexplainable experience I've ever had took place a couple of hours up the road in rural Mississippi.

Going into my senior year of high school, my parents finished building their dream home on family owned land. Their home sat at the end of a short road with no other homes. The only other thing on this road was a cemetery - an extremely old cemetery. I've been told it predates the Civil War, but I can't be sure. The older headstones have no dates carved on them.

One weekend, I did what teens do while their parents are out of town, and had friends over to drink, and act like idiots. I've always respected cemeteries: viewing them as sacred grounds reserved for those who have already put in their time on earth. However, with the influence of drinks and friends, I decided to show my bravery by removing my shirt, running through the cemetery, and pouring splashes of liquor on the graves. I tell you this because nothing ever happened before that night.

Afterwards, I started experiencing sleep paralysis—which I'd never had before, or since I moved out of that house. It wasn't like most cases that I've heard. I would be completely alert, watching tv in bed, and then suddenly become unable to move or speak. I would hear low, urgent whispers coming from behind my head on my left side. This would happen for around thirty seconds or so, then I could move and speak like normal.

Then, little things began happening. My TV would suddenly come on in the middle of the night; pictures would be crooked on the wall when I woke up in the morning; I would see shadows dart past my windows. I know it all seems minor, but combined with the sleep paralysis, it had me on edge.

I moved out shortly after graduation, and it all just stopped.

A few years later, my now wife and I went to visit my parents for a weekend. I'd told my wife of all the strangeness that I experienced at the house, but she thought it was all in my mind.

Close to dark, my parents ran to town to get last minute items to cook for our last evening there. Standing in the kitchen with the window open, we stopped talking because we heard a noise. It was unmistakable: the clip clop of horse hooves and the squeaking of wheels being pulled behind it. We looked out the window and saw dust—as if someone had driven down the dirt drive. We quickly ran outside to see....nothing. No dust, no horse, no car (other than our own; which was parked exactly where we left it).

My wife no longer thinks all those past experiences I'd had were in my mind; and she prefers my parents to come to our place if they want to visit.

Anything Ghost Show, Episode #245

Chapter Five

Hotels

The spirit-world around this world of sense
Floats like an atmosphere, and everywhere
Wafts through these earthly mists and vapours dense
A vital breath of more ethereal air.

(Poem Continues in Chapter 6)

Stories Surrounding Stockton on the Tees, England
Lee (U.K.)

I live in a northern English town called Stockton on Tees. The Tees is the river that flows through the region. It is a very old town, indeed: our market dates back to at least 1100 AD; and the castle in our town was ordered destroyed by Oliver Cromwell.

In the past the river was a very important and busy part of town—and you can well imagine the scenes and lives that have played out there over hundreds and hundreds of years. In the nineteenth century the press gangs arrived at the river area, looking to kidnap men and force them to work at sea as slaves.

1780: Press Gang. Capturing men to fight for the navy or military (Created: 31 December 1779)

Many a tragedy has unfolded there due to the dangerous waters. Mothers would keep their children away from the river by telling them the legend of Jenny Green Teeth: an evil spirit that lurked on the banks of the river looking for children and lonely travelers to pounce upon and drag into the filthy water—drowning them before feasting on their bodies!

Another creature said to lurk along the River Tees is Peg Powler: said to be an evil fresh water mermaid who would lure the curious to the rocks—enchant them with her song, and then drag them to a watery death.

Along a very lonely and deserted path by the river stood an old cottage. The cottage was used by smugglers and had tunnels running from its cellar to the river bank. Many sailors, passing by the cottage to make his way to his digs (his room), perhaps on a lonely wind swept night, have reported eerie sounds and lights at the cottage. Were the spooky goings on set up by smugglers to keep the curious away? We will never know.

Our airport (Teesside Airport) was originally known as Goosepool Aerodrome during WWII. The airport had many attached buildings including an officer's quarters. From this airport, Brave British, Canadian and Polish airmen would launch devastating bombing raids on Germany. During one such raid, a Canadian pilot tragically crashed his plane and was killed shortly after take off. His plane smashed into the officer's housing block (which many years later was converted into a plush hotel).

Over the years several pilots and aircrew have reported seeing a ghostly airman dressed in full flying gear in the hotel—as well as in one of the giant hangers. Was this the brave Canadian pilot that lost his life so long ago?

Anything Ghost Show, Episode #168

Stranger at the Strater
Greg (Michigan, U.S.)

When I was in my early twenties, I worked at a historic hotel in Durango Colorado. As with any old hotel, there were plenty of stories of paranormal activity. Ghost hunters sought it out regularly; and there were always ghost tours during Halloween.

The building itself looms fairly large, in what is otherwise a small, historical main-street downtown. Upon entering the hotel, your eyes are drawn to countless ornate fixtures everywhere. Then there are the wonderful collections of antique furniture; and the numerous glass cases in the common areas containing mining artifacts (black and white photos, deeds, minerals and all the tools of a turn of the century mining town).

Many stories among the staff involved supernatural occurrences. People reported unexplained sounds such as footsteps and disembodied voices early in the morning; chairs sliding on floors; missing items; temperature changes, and the like—pretty much every kind of classic haunting experience you'd expect to hear at such a place.

I have always balanced my curiosity with a healthy dose of skepticism, and went about my job without much thought of ever seeing or hearing anything out of the ordinary. I felt it was just a privilege to work in a place with such a rich history. I never actually expected anything to happen to me; but I don't think anyone is ever truly prepared for these kinds of experiences.

One of my duties was to prepare rooms for special events. The room I was in this particular morning was known as the "Pullman Room." So named because it was long and narrow—like a Pullman train-car. It was located downstairs in what was one of the oldest parts of the hotel—meaning, it had been there since the late 1800's (prior to renovations in the newer part of the hotel). The Pullman Room had long mirrored walls running the length of the room on either side, lending it the effect of seeming bigger than it actually was. It was a very nice room, but it always seemed dim even with the lights on.

I showed up in the morning and began setting tables for a wedding that was taking place later in the week. As said before, there was a story about every part of that hotel. The Pullman Room was known to be haunted by a man who was shot over some kind of business dealing involving a silver claim. Despite my skeptical attitude, what I saw next was absolutely unexplainable, and is burned indelibly into my memory.

I was going around to each table setting flatware, when out of the corner of my eye I saw someone walking between the tables. I looked over to see who it was (because I thought I was alone). There are several doors in the room, so I figured someone must've entered without me noticing. But when I looked over, there was no one there. I shrugged it off to my eyes playing tricks on me and continued with my task.

A moment later, I heard the clinking of a coffee cup against a saucer (as though someone had bumped into one of the tables). I turned around, sure that I would see someone this time. Again, my eyes met nothing but an empty room. I tried to determine which table the noise had come from, but couldn't. At that point, I began to feel a little on edge, and said to myself, "Okay. One more weird thing like that, and I'm outta here!"

Working quickly now, but focusing hard on the reflection of one of the mirrored walls, I saw what was clearly the lower half of a person in period clothing. It was walking no more than ten feet away: two legs in high black boots and tan pants—the torso was not visible at all! I saw the legs take four steps, and then I dropped what was in my hands and headed straight for the door! I had the chills and felt like a little kid running upstairs from the basement.

Rather than explaining why I was leaving, I said I wasn't feeling well and that I'd be back to finish later in the day. I ended up having someone else finish setting up the room.

It wasn't the last time I was alone in the hotel, and not the last time I experienced something unexplained there. I was like a spooked house cat from then on.

Anything Ghost Show, Episode #232

The Little Girl at the Top of the Stairs
Cas (U.K.)

When I was sixteen years old, I lived in a sort of youth hostel for young adults. I lived on the first floor and shared a "cluster" with three other people. This hostel housed up to forty-seven residents and there was always staff on site (support workers and security) to look out for us 24/7.

We all knew each other at this place (and there were a whole host of characters living there), but one thing was common for all of us...the stairs!

The building had four floors, including the ground floor. To reach the upper floors, there were stairs or a lift—but the lift was shut off at night. Very soon after moving in, I wouldn't go to any floor above the first when the lift wasn't on. The reason was that when you ascended the stairs (between the first and second floor), terror ensued—everyone scrambled up those stairs! I'm don't mean grabbing the rail and running up; I mean trying to move so fast that you were using your hands to drag yourself up the stairs. It felt like something was chasing you—and there was no way you were going to let it catch you!

After a few months of this (it was the middle of the day), and I went up to the fourth floor to visit a friend. The lift was off that day for maintenance, so I had no choice but to take the stairs. Like clock work, I walked up the first flight, scrambled up the second and then was at ease for the third flight.

Once I reach the fourth floor, I saw a little girl standing at the entrance door. The girl couldn't have been more than seven years old. She had long hair (kind of a dirty blonde colour), a little white summer dress with tiny blue flowers all over it, and bare feet.

At the youth hostel, you needed a swipe card to go through the door on each level, so I wasn't about to let this little girl in (I would get into a lot of trouble: because visiting children were only allowed in the lounge area downstairs). So, I stood at the top of the stairs and tried to coax the girl down.

"Hey little one, are you lost?" I said.

I got nothing back—not even recognition that she had heard me.

"Are you looking for your mummy or daddy?"

Still nothing.

"You know you can't be up here right? We need to go back downstairs. Come on, I'll take you."

I put out my hand for her to take.

At that moment, she turned her head in my direction but was looking over my shoulder (as opposed to looking at me).

Then she screamed a high pitch and terrified type of scream!

I jumped outta my skin and looked behind me. There, in the brightly lit staircase, up in the corner on the ceiling, I could see what looked like a shadow; but it was denser, and spread out from the corner across to the ceiling.

I was suddenly engulfed in the feeling I got whenever I tried to take the stairs between first and second. I turned to the girl (ready to pick her up and run down the stairs)...and she was gone.

I looked back over my shoulder and the shadow was gone, too.

There is no way that little girl could've gone through the door—she needed to swipe a card—and the door was very heavy (owing to it being a fire safety door).

There was no way she could've gotten past me, as I was blocking the stairs.

When I recalled this to one of the staff, they said that when they did their nightly checks, they would take the fire escape stairs to reach each floor...as they had seen that same girl playing on the stairs, or simply standing at the fourth floor door.

She isn't the first I've seen, but she was certainly the first child I have seen—and it freaked me out!

Anything Ghost Show, Episode #248

53

Chapter Six

Houses

Our little lives are kept in equipoise
By opposite attractions and desires;
The struggle of the instinct that enjoys,
And the more noble instinct that aspires.

(Poem Continues in Chapter 7)

1930's Bungalow Renovations
Lesley (Southampton, U.K.)

The events I'm about to tell you, happened when we moved into a 1930's bungalow...the first significant event, happened early on.

We had decided to build a small extension onto our property to extend the kitchen (as I love to cook, and the current kitchen was a little small), and we hired an architect to scope out what would be needed. When he arrived, he walked into the hallway, hesitated for a second, and then carried on. That was followed by some discussion about what we were looking for in regard to the new build. After that, we walked through the house.

Just as we were walking to the kitchen, there was a huge crashing sound from behind us. We both ducked instinctively, and then quickly stepped back into the hallway. The loft hatch was swinging to-and-fro—it had opened on its own...or, so it seemed.

The architect walked back into the hallway and looked curiously up at the aperture. He made some mention of a strong breeze affecting the pressure, and noted that may have caused the door to swing open. He then asked if there was an access ladder, because he wanted to take a look up in the attic. The house—having been somewhat neglected—didn't have a built in ladder, so I fetched him a stepladder.

Then I heard him exclaim from behind me that the loft hatch had crashed down so violently that the wall was dented (in fact, that dent can still be seen today). I laughed nervously, and made a joke about how we must be stirring up the resident ghost.

After he poked his head up in the loft space, and looked around the house a little more, we sat down and chatted about what he thought we could do. Afterward, he showed me a few preliminary sketches, and left.

At that point, we had only lived in the house for a few months. There was nothing remarkable: it was just a 1930's detached bungalow on an ordinary suburban street—and before the incident with the loft hatch and the architect, all had been fine.

After that though, well, that's when things began to get interesting.

Building work began in early June. The builder, Frank, was working outside digging the foundations for the extension. Since he was our neighbor, I was quite happy to give him the back door key when we went to work—with instructions to help himself to tea and coffee (he never did, though, and it wasn't until much later that I found out why).

On one occasion, when Frank was explaining what he'd done that day, when the loft hatch once again came crashing down, and we both ducked. Frank, after a puzzled look, assured me that he'd fix that hatch for me; and he put a sturdy bolt in place to ensure that it wouldn't happen again—which it didn't.

As the building work got under way, odd things began to happen on a regular basis. The house began to develop an atmosphere. What does that mean? It's hard to explain:

- I began to feel awkward when padding around in the dark (if I woke up in the night);
- I began to notice odd noises in other areas of the house;
- Things that had been misplaced turned up in weird places;
- The "breeze" that the architect had noted (when the loft hatch sprung open), became more obvious—whatever the weather outside.

In short, the house became vaguely uncomfortable to be in—particularly when I was on my own.

On one occasion, my daughter was shocked to see a dark shape (like a figure) standing in a doorway. As she watched, it ducked and moved out of sight. The only other person in the house at the time had been reading in another room, and it wasn't him.

Naturally, I tried to dismiss it, and to think rationally about what was going on. The odd noises could be put down to the building work, and the stresses and strains being put on the fabric of the building; as for the stray breezes, as for the misplaced items turning up in odd places…well, I'm sure you can think of your own explanation for that. I managed to dismiss the whole thing for weeks.

One night, I woke suddenly because I heard a crashing noise coming from the kitchen. Frank had been working on the extension out there, and the next day he was due to knock down the old inner wall. The only things left in the kitchen by that time were a counter, a small table and chair, and the gas cooker. Puzzled and a little alarmed, I headed to the kitchen and switched on the lights to see what had fallen. The chair (that had been tucked under the table), was lying on its side—quite a ways from the table. The kitchen was cold—to the extent that I could see my breath as I looked around. The strange thing was that despite the oddness of the situation, I felt very calm—not in the least scared.

I'd wondered for some time if the work on the house may have stirred up a ghost. I found the idea intriguing, so I decided to speak to the "potential ghost" just to see what would happen.

"I'm sorry if I've disturbed you with the building work. Do you object? You must admit that the house is rather small—and I like to cook. I need a bigger kitchen."

Nothing—no response.

The only thing that happened was that the kitchen got slightly warmer.

"Look," I said. "It's going to happen. I can't stop the building work at this stage. And who knows? You might like it when it's finished! How about you stop messing about, and wait and see?"

Again, there was no response.

Sighing, I shut off the light and turned to leave the kitchen. As I did so, I heard a slight clinking sound. Quickly, I turned the kitchen lights back on, and saw that the row of mugs hanging from cup-hooks over the counter were swinging gently backwards and forwards.

I smiled, "Good-night, then."

Well, all that happened a while ago now. The building work is all done—and I love my nice, big kitchen. If I did have a ghost in my house who was objecting to the building work, she's generally very quiet these days.

Everything that happened was a bit odd, but perfectly explainable, I suppose. Except for one last, odd thing…

Frank, the builder, never did come inside the house when I wasn't there. And it wasn't until very recently that I found out why.

I asked him the other day.

"Ah," he said. "Your mother was always there—and I didn't like to just walk in."

"My mother?!" I exclaimed—startled, to say the least.

"Yes! The elderly lady in the yellow cardigan. She used to watch me work sometimes—through the door. Mostly, she just sat in your kitchen."

"And what made you think she was mother?" I asked (more than a little confused at that point).

"Well, I don't know really. Just an assumption, I suppose. She's there a lot." He replied.

My mother would never just enter our house without being invited. And I'm sure she would have spoken to Frank if she came over—and she confirmed that when I asked her.

I decided not to enlighten Frank, though: some things are better left unsaid. And besides, we may want to ask Frank to help out with building-work again one day.

Anything Ghost Show, Episode #145

Spooky Happenings in a New York Apartment

Lisa (New York, U.S.)

A few years ago, I moved into an apartment building on the edge of New York City. Contrary to the city's restless vibe and energized streets, my little neighborhood was actually quite peaceful. When night came, everything was very quiet and still—even my neighbors were quiet. The building was over eighty years old, and, believe it or not, looked a bit like an old haunted castle (with its medieval-looking stonework, archways, and courtyard).

Ever since moving in, there have been some odd happenings inside my small apartment that have given me reason to wonder….could it possibly be haunted?

My apartment needed some TLC, so there was a lot of drilling and hammering before moving in—and you know what they say about renovations in old buildings: it can stir up the spirits!

First, there was the teddy bear.

It was a medium-sized bear that for months sat against the wall on top of my bookcase. Everything was solid and sturdy. The bookcase was even attached to the wall. Nothing could possibly have jostled that bear! But one night, as I was peacefully walking down the hall (that lead to the bookcase), the bear flew off the top shelf and onto the floor in front of me! I was stunned, and tried to recreate the scenario, returning the bear to the top shelf, and inspecting the floor, wall, and bookcase—everything was as sturdy as ever and the bear did not budge again.

Another night, I was alone and taking a bath. Everything was very quiet (I have no pets or children). My bathroom door was open. Suddenly, I could hear what sounded like the crunching and rustling of plastic bags out in the living room area. I was terrified: "Was somebody in my apartment? Was it a mouse? Impossible!"

I listened to this sound intently for a minute or two and then it stopped. It was undoubtedly inside my apartment. Frozen in place, I continued to wait and listen…then the crunching and rustling started again! After about a minute, it completely stopped, and I finally summoned up the nerve to venture out of the bathroom. There was nothing and no one. Nothing had tipped over. And there was no possibility of a mouse—everything was spick and span, with no openings anywhere.

There have been more inexplicable occurrences (too many to list):

- An empty plastic juice bottle tipping over on the kitchen table when no one was near it;
- Pine cones popping out of a seasonal decoration, left undisturbed for months on a heavy table;

- A ceiling lamp that flashed on—then off—in a peculiar way, which never happened before or since.
- Then there's that occasional cold spot in the kitchen—which is nowhere near a window, door, or any other opening.

Sure, it's easy to read into strange events like these, but I have yet to find any explanations. Can spirits or impressions from the past linger in a house or building?—Science has yet to unravel that mystery. I don't know the history of my apartment, so I can only speculate. But, when night comes, I will continue to leave the hallway light on....just in case.

Anything Ghost Show, Episode #229

Haunted Childhood Home
Daniel (Canada)

Ghosts have always been apart of my family's life. For as far back as I can remember, my father would always tell my two sisters and I that if we ever saw or felt a ghost/spirit (and did not want to be scared or frightened by it), all we had to do was welcome the spirit with kind words. My father and mother were not scared of anything paranormal. They would go see a physic every year, and she would always tell them the same thing: we lived in a house full of ghosts.

This physic had never been to our house, nor knew where we lived; but she knew that we lived with many different ghosts in our home. This did not scare any of my family, and we have all had our experiences with these ghosts:
- My eldest sister would hear them talking and whispering to her almost daily—unfortunately, she was very frightened by this, and started imagining herself standing in a white light. Soon after that, the voices stopped bothering her. She has never heard them since.
- My middle sister had every door in the entire house slam shut on a clear sunny day. Not a window open to cause a draft, but every door slammed shut. She followed in my eldest sister's path of imagining a white light. Nothing has happened to her since.
- My mom had one of the most interesting experiences. She was coming home from the grocery store, my sisters and I were at school and dad was at work. She had her arms full of bags and was fumbling with the keys. She managed to open the door. As soon as the door opened, she clearly heard the voice of a man say, "Hello Elizabeth." She promptly closed the door and locked it again, walked away from the house, and waited outside for a few minutes to calm down. When she went back in for the second time, no voices were there.

My story on the other hand, was very different. It took place a few months after my grandfather had passed away in November 2011. My parents' room was at the far top corner of the house, and my room was on the far opposite from their room. It was about 2:30 in the morning, and I was having the weirdest dreams: dreams that people were standing over me and telling me to wake up. I was able to wake myself. I looked around my room and saw very clearly a boy about five years old, dressed in blue jean overalls; he was sitting next to a five-year -old girl wearing a white nightgown and sitting on my desk.

I sat up on the edge of my bed looking straight at them. They looked at one another, and then straight back to me. I was astonished at what was in front of me. I rubbed my eyes to make sure I was awake. But I was awake, and seeing just fine. I asked them calmly, "Why are you here? Can I help you with anything?"

They once again looked at each other. The little boy looked back towards me and pointed at my chest, and they both vanished.

I raced up stairs to my parents' room, woke them up, and explained what had just taken place. Dad assured me that they were there just to say hello, and nothing more. He thought it could have been my grandfather saying goodbye, or he could have just popped in for a visited in the same way he did from time to time when he was alive. Either way, I was too spooked to sleep in that room for the rest of the night.

Nothing much has happened in my parent's house since then. Every now and then when I'm over for dinner, I still get the feeling that we (the living), are not the only ones in the house.

Anything Ghost Show, Episode #229

Curious Incidents on Lathrop Street
Thom (U.S.)

We've had a few odd experiences. Maybe they have non-paranormal explanations, but we like to think there might be something going on around here.

My girlfriend and I live in a small cottage house on the outskirts of the German Village near Downtown Columbus OH. Most of the houses in the area are old. Ours was built in the 1890's. The house creaks and groans constantly and it never ceases to be at least a little moody. There's a tall wood fence that encloses the small property. Part of the fence is a heavy wood gate that bangs rhythmically when it's windy. It's just the two of us at the house and our two dogs.

One of our neighbors has shared a story, with us, about a man who lived in a long-gone shack somewhere on the block. This man allegedly hung himself in the shack and now haunts the block wandering from yard to yard and house to house. We think we caught this ghost on camera one evening after a date. We recently acquired an old classic car and had just taken it out for our date. When we returned home from the date I got out my phone, hoping for a cool nighttime pic of the car. We were in the alleyway that runs alongside our house. I snapped maybe a half dozen pics. When reviewing them we found this large green orb. It was particularly odd, because when I took the pics I was standing in one spot and the pics were of the same area. The orb appeared in a different place in each pic. In the first, it appeared further away with the car clearly between us and it. In the last, it was clearly between us and the car. We could find no obvious explanation for it's appearance.

The more interesting stories took place within our home, before we adopted our second dog.

The house is open, essentially one room, with the living room space at the front of the house, the dining room in the middle and the kitchen at the rear. The back door is in the kitchen and opens up onto a deck and small yard where our dog, Pilot, plays and does his business. I need to mention, one of the first things we did when we adopted Pilot was train him to ring a set of bells when he needs to do his business. These bells hang on the doorknob of the back door. We spend most of our evenings at the front of the house in the living room watching television, our backs to the dining room and kitchen.

This one evening my girlfriend and I were particularly tired. Zuz works long hours and at the time I was working full-time and going to school full-time. Like most evenings we couldn't get out of our work clothes and into our pajamas fast enough. We had just sat down in the living room to eat dinner and watch television when we heard Pilot's bells jingle. It was a good confident jingle. He really needed out. No delay. With all the energy I could muster I turned and asked Zuz if she would let Pilot out. She gave me a strange look. I was sure she was going to decline and insist I handle it. Instead she replied, "Pilot's right here." She leaned back to reveal him sitting next to her on the couch. As confidently as I was able I ventured to the kitchen to investigate. There was no clear explanation for the bell jingling.

A year later, again, we were spending time in the living room when we heard a loud THUD come from the kitchen. We both hopped up to investigate and found a wine bottle rolling around on the floor. Our small wine rack was kept in an open cabinet a couple of feet above the sink. It appeared as though the bottle had fallen some six feet from the rack to the floor and missed the sink on its way down -- all without breaking. There was no clear explanation for how the bottle came to be on the floor or why it hadn't broken.

About that same time, Pilot began acting very strangely. He was six or seven years old at the time and had been part of our family since he was seven weeks old. He spent almost all of his time with us wherever we were in the house. If we were watching television, he would be right there with us in the living room. If we were cooking, he would be in the kitchen. If we were sleeping, he was on the bed.

One evening when we were again in the living room watching television, Pilot, hopped up, obviously spooked, and ran out of the room. We found him hiding under the dining room table. No amount of coaxing could get him to come out. I had to pull him out, physically, and hold him tightly to keep him with us in the living room. If I let him go he would immediately run back to hide under the table. We were sure he would join us for bed when it was time to sleep. He did not. I was so worried about him that I slept under the table with him that night. At that time, I worked in a dog-friendly office. Pilot came to work with me every day. His behavior was totally normal at the office, but as soon as we returned home he was back under the table. This went on for a few days before we took him to the vet to make sure his health was okay. The vet had no explanation for his behavior. We got him one of those therapy vests and a special scent diffuser to help calm him down. Thankfully, after another week, he returned to his normal behavior.

Anything Ghost Show, Episode #234

Shadow People and the Boy Ghost
Darian (New Mexico, U.S.)

I have always believed, from a young age, that my house was haunted. Odd things would happen that never made any sense: alarm clocks would go off without being plugged in; doors would shut by themselves; I even saw my dog (who had just passed away) lying on the couch, then disappear. All of this over the years never really bothered me growing up. My dad always told us it was the house settling.

One night when I was about fifteen, I had fallen asleep (and it had only been about 45 minutes since I had actually dozed off); I had been tossing and turning, until I turned over towards my closest. I had woken up enough to see that there was a short black figure of a boy standing in front of me. I was able to distinguish the figure due to the light from my clock and DVD player. He was just standing there, until I fixed up the reality and screamed for my parents. It then disappeared. My parents believed I was dreaming, so I chalked it up to that.

However, a few months later when I saw a black figure once again. This time he was standing over my bed and staring at me. This happened over and over (sometimes weeks apart or months) for the rest of the three years that I lived in there.

When these figures started appearing to me, my brother had commented about seeing figures walk past his doorway at night towards my room—or standing over his bed. Sometimes, immediately after seeing these figures pass his room, he'd hear me scream. That was when I knew I wasn't the only one really seeing these figures.

The more active these figures got, the more odd happenings would occur.

My parents would always lock my two dogs up in the cage in the back room before going out, but sometimes my mom would forget to lock them up; she would come home and they would be in the cage with the door closed—even though she knew she didn't put them away; the laundry soap would fly off the washer in front of my mom; food would randomly fall from our pantry—it got to the point to where everyone had seen something...except my dad.

My dad lit some sage in our house, and the happenings diminished quite a bit. But the last couple months living at that house, I saw the figures more frequently—and eventually I was unable to sleep because of it.

I was going to start college the summer after my graduation, and had already started moving things into my friend's house in Albuquerque. On the night I moved all my things into his house, I knew the paranormal was at his place, too. I had been sleeping for several hours before, and I heard a small thud and woke up. I turned over to face the wall and saw a tall, blonde haired, blue-eyed boy with orange shorts standing in front of me. At first, I assumed it was my roommate (since he was tall and had blonde hair). I immediately asked his what he was doing? Within seconds, the figure vanished.

Over the past five months of living with my friend in Albuquerque, nothing of significance happened, until a few weeks ago. I woke up in the middle of the night to a hand squeezing my wrist and shaking it up and down. I panicked and ran to my roommate's sister. I finished out the night sleeping in her room, and talking about all the ghostly happenings we had both experienced. I had told her about the figure of the blonde haired boy in my room, and she told me that before she was born, her parents had a five-year-old child who died of a certain disease. I came to find out that this little boy had blonde hair, and blue eyes and had passed away in that house.

Anything Ghost Show, Episode #230

Haunted House and Black Magic in Venezuela
Maria (The Hague, Netherlands)

I'm originally from Venezuela, South America. Although I haven't lived in my home country for a while, the story I'm going to narrate happened when I was a teenager, and living with my parents in the city of Barcelona, Venezuela.

We moved several times when I was a child. My parents were enthusiastic entrepreneurs that invested most of their money in all kind of venues, with little or no interest in settle down in one place. Therefore, I grew up living in different places, nothing out of the ordinary, just old houses in an old colonial city by the Caribbean Sea.

The year was 1988 and our new destination was a simple two-story house that was probably in the seventies. The disrepair was obvious, but I didn't care: I knew it wasn't our home, and we wouldn't be staying there for as long (as my parents would find something better). Nevertheless, this house was different—even though we didn't notice it in the beginning.

At first, it seemed as the other houses we had lived in: a regular building; a concrete structure with no personality; no signs of paranormal activity; just another place to spend our lives as we kept enduring the endless cycle of moving.

However, as soon as we got inside of the house, and started to move our stuff in, we noticed something wasn't quite right. The first thing we noticed was black candle wax in the corners of every room; and then the little wooden crosses over the frames of every single door. We all saw this, and although thought it was weird, we just brushed it off (maybe because we were a pragmatic oriented family with no interest in the paranormal and no knowledge about witchcraft; or maybe because we were in the need for a place to live, and didn't have the chance to pay attention to the warning signs). Nevertheless, we just kept things running.

The house, or whatever was inside, didn't wait long to let us know that this was ITS' place—and we weren't welcomed! The first night we spent there, while we were watching TV in the living room, the faucets on the upper level bathroom went on by themselves (with no possible logical explanation), and didn't stop until we gathered the courage to go up and turn them off. Again, we overlooked the incident, and came up with the best answer we could think of: this was an old house with a lot of things that needed repairs.

Then it came: the nightmares.

I started to have recurrent dreams about people I didn't know: they would be looking through the windows from the outside, and trying to get into the house—as if they wanted to find something that had been lost a long time ago. I couldn't have a normal night's sleep for a long time—always having a heavy sense of fear, uneasiness (this was during daylight or nighttime). The atmosphere was never peaceful, and it was as if something was constantly about to happened. I was in my teenage years at that time, and I spent long sleepless nights reading or writing—too afraid of going to bed because of the dreams.

By that time, I started to have a strange feeling of living in a house with an alternate reality: things worked in a different logic than the world outside—a powerful logic that we couldn't participate in, and could only be affected by. The house seemed to have a life on its own, and we were just mere objects to be moved according to its disposition.

One particular night, I was finally in a deep sleep when I was awakened by a terrifying sensation that I wasn't alone in the room. I opened my eyes to scan the room, and immediately saw a tall lady standing by my bed. She was dressed completely in black. She had pale white skin, dark short hair, and was looking at me with profound black eyes—without moving or saying a word. I remember trying to leave my bed, but was unable to do it because I was wrapped so tightly in the sheets. I finally freed myself from the sheets, and in absolute terror, I ran yelling to my parents (waking up the entire house).

Since that experience—and because of it—I have had a long history of sleep disorders that have affected me in the years that followed (intermingled with depression).

A couple years after all of those events, another house came along and I was more than happy to move. After we moved, my mother told me something she knew but had never revealed: they didn't have money to rent a better house, and took that one at a really low price—even knowing that the previous tenant had practiced black magic.

The house hasn't been occupied in a long time—I assume because of its haunted history.

We never went back to that place again.

I ended up leaving the city to go to college, and eventually I left the country. But over the years, I have come to the realization that a part of me died in that house, and things weren't the same for me after living there. I know now that my later fascination with the paranormal has been a way for me to cope with that experience: a way to understand that there are dimensions beyond our knowledge and sometimes they overlap to affect us...for good or bad.

Anything Ghost Show, Episode #239

Creepy Russian Childhood House

Slava (Russia)

From my birth, until I was nine years old, I lived in a three-bedroom house that I shared with my two sisters, brother and my mom (my father had passed away when I was a little over a year old).

The house had a strange design to it. Two of the sides shared a thin wall with two other "houses" (as if a large mansion had been divided into smaller houses that were still connected). It was almost like an apartment, except that we had a fenced in front and side yard. The exterior of the house was made from dark red brick.

One of the most memorable things about this house was that I was always afraid of being alone in the house. I constantly felt that there was something hiding in the walls—something that was there long before my parents or me.

The first experience I remember happened on a warm summer night. That night I woke up to go to the bathroom (that was located on opposite side of the house from our bedroom); a long hallway separated us from the bathroom. I didn't want to turn on the light in the hallway, as it was very bright; plus, the streetlight that was coming through the window at the end of the hallway and that was enough for me to safely walk to the bathroom.

As I was making my way down the hallway, I slowed down as I was passing the kitchen. For a moment, I felt someone there. I could not see much, except for some dim light reflecting on refrigerator, and an empty olive oil glass bottle. After a quick glance towards the kitchen, I decided to resume my normal speed and continued my way towards the bathroom. At that very moment the empty olive oil bottle flew off the table—as if someone had purposely knocked it down! The idea that someone or something was hiding in the kitchen and had been watching me, made me run straight to the bathroom and lock the door.

It took about thirty minutes for me to get back all my courage and make my way back to the bedroom.

Another occurrence took place sometime later.

One night, I was awakened by a sound of someone running in the living room. I looked at the gap between the door of my bedroom and the floor, and I could not see any light coming from the living room. The running continued for about five minutes, and then just stopped.

The next morning my brother came to me and said that he spotted something strange in the living room. When I walked to the living room I saw child size dirty footprints on bottom of one of the walls. Instead of shoe prints, these looked like a child's dirty socks had made prints on the wall. The footprints continued up to the middle of the wall and all the up towards the ceiling.

I told my brother that the night before I had heard running in our living room, to which he replied that he had also heard running a few times before.

Other occurrences included: cabinets in the kitchen opening by themselves, and knocks on the door that separated the sun room from the rest of the house.

In the beginning, I mentioned that my father had passed away when I was little over a year old. Well, one night he came to me in a nightmare. In my dream, I woke up in my bed. As I was getting out, I noticed that there was a table right in front of my bed, and on that table was a coffin. The coffin was dressed in red fabric (which in Russia means a young or a middle aged person had passed away). For some reason, I knew right away that it was my father. I got up little closer to the coffin. At that very moment my father rose up from the coffin and began to stretch his arms towards me as if he wanted to grab me. I jumped out the bed and tried to run away. At the moment my father nearly reached me with his hands, I woke up.

I don't remember how much time passed before I fell asleep again, but I remember that I laid there frozen—not making a single sound or moving a muscle.

My mother never talked about my father; his death remains a partial mystery to me.

While living there, my mother forbade us from going into the small room located in the basement. As long as I can remember, there had been a big pad lock on the door of that room. In the past few months, with the help of my brother, I've begun doing some research on that home. I found that it was not built in 1950's or 1960's as I'd first thought, it was built in 1850's.

In addition, the house was part of a much bigger house that was later divided into four separate living spaces. I don't know much about who built the house, but it was most likely built by a wealthy family around October of the 1917 revolution—and the owners were forcefully evicted from the house by Bolsheviks. There were no records of what happened to the family after the eviction.

My grandmother once told me that the people who lived there before my parents had a baby; however, the newborn disappeared. Rumors circulated that the mother of the newborn baby buried it alive—presumably because she could not take care of it.

It's been over a decade since I've seen my childhood house. After my family moved out, no one else moved in. The last I heard, the house had been transformed into storage for nearby businesses. Part of me really wants to go back to the house and look around—in the hope of finding some answers about my childhood paranormal experiences.

Anything Ghost Show, Episode #244

Haunted Indiana Duplex
Chris (Logan, Utah)

I was living in Westville, Indiana in 2013, and I was between jobs. My girlfriend and I were renting an old house that was split into a duplex by the floor. We had the first floor, and a young couple had the second floor. I would guess the house was built in the early 1900's. There were two entrances to our floor: one was in the back and went directly into the kitchen; the other was the front door (that was never used). That door opened up to the main stairs and went to the second floor. There were also French doors next to the stairs that went right into our living room. These French doors were kept locked at all times to keep some privacy between us and the other tenants.

The first thing that seemed strange in the house was that my girlfriend and I (who normally slept until 8 AM), started waking up at exactly 5 AM every morning. This was weird because we both stayed up late on normal nights and this only gave us about four hours of sleep. For some reason we would both wake up and just have an urge to be awake—like we were meant to be awake for some reason. After a while, we got used to this and just started our day earlier and going to bed sooner.

After about a month of living in this house, my girlfriend was at work and I left to go to the gym. I returned home about an hour later. As I walked up to the door I could hear our dog making very strange noises from inside the house. When I opened the door, our dog was cowering in the corner—crying in fear. This was a 110-pound old English sheep dog, and he wasn't afraid of anything. I quickly noticed that something was wrong because there was about an inch of water covering the floor of the house. As I walked around, I found that there were five random spots on the ceiling from which water was basically raining. The water was not coming from a spot where pipes were located (or where anything water-related would have been on the second floor).

I got together with my girlfriend and the landlord to figure out what was going on. We shut the water to the house off, but the "rain" continued for another hour. The landlord never found a leak anywhere—or any logical reason for the water. Nothing was flooding on the second floor, and the water was just in the five random spots throughout the house.

After that incident things got really strange. The French doors that opened up to the main stairwell for the house suddenly became a place of fear for all of us. Our dog wouldn't go near them; we never wanted to look at them—and even ended up putting a desk in front of them to cover the door. For some reason, we felt like something was on the other side of that door in the stairwell; and we didn't want to acknowledge, or let whatever it was, into our house.

This last thing, still gives me get goose bumps.

It was the middle of the night and we were sleeping. We keep the room pitch black and always have the sheep dog on the floor by the bed. I was dead asleep. Suddenly, I had the feeling that something was in the bed with us. I could feel it moving up my legs. I bolted straight up in bed, looked in front of me where I felt this thing, and saw a creature that I cannot even describe. It was standing on my legs and looking at me. My first thought was to scream. But I swung my right arm at it as hard as I possibly could—I will never forget the feeling of my fist making direct contact with this thing, and knocking it off the bed.

At that moment, my scream (plus me punching) woke my girlfriend, and she jumped up and turned the lights on. Our dog was going crazy barking and running around the room. I explained what happened and she immediately believed me, because of how intensely scared I was.

We looked all over for this thing, but never found a trace of it.

After that, things were never the same in the house.

We couldn't sleep—we were constantly on alert. We kept all of the blinds open and lights on during the day so we would have as much light as possible in the house. Because of that, one day I noticed a man walking back and forth on the sidewalk in front of our house for over an hour. We really thought this was weird, so I went out to confront the guy.

The man asked me if I lived in the house. Next he asked if I had been experiencing any weird things.

I said yes, and asked why he would ask something like that.

He said that he had lived there in the past, and had several experiences that still haunted him to this day. This got me really nervous, but I had to know what happened to him.

He said that he lived on the second floor, and would use the stairwell to leave each morning for work. For some reason, even though he didn't have to leave until 7 AM, he started waking up at 5 AM every day. When he would leave down the stairs, he always got a creepy feeling so would hurry down the stairs and out the door. One morning he was at the top of the stairs and looked down to see a ghostly woman in white walking up towards him. He ran the other way and out the other door to the house. This continued to happen every morning until he decided to never try the stairs again.

I then told him how that stairwell had been really freaking us out, and went on to explain the raining in the house experience. He stopped me in the middle of the story, and said I bet I can name the exact five places it was raining. To my astonishment he named all of them. He said that those places on the second floor always made strange sounds and were colder than other places in the house. He tried his best to avoid walking through them.

I thanked him for telling me about his experiences, and then went inside to retell everything to my girlfriend. This was enough for us to decide to move out. We already knew 100% that what we were experiencing was strange, but after having another person we didn't even know tell us the same things, we just couldn't handle it.

Anything Ghost Show, Episode #227

The Little Burned Boy at the GI House
Leta (Greeneville, Tennessee)

I was born and raised in Wyandotte, Michigan. We lived in a small house built in 1947 (it was part of the GI bill to provide housing for the returning veterans of WWII). During the day the house would be quiet and cozy, but this would disappear as soon as evening began.

At an early age, I began seeing shadow figures all about the house; faces on the walls; whispered conversations; the TV would turn off and on; and shadow beings that would stare at me.

Leta at age nine, standing in front of the GI house.

But the most terrifying figure of all was the little burned boy who lived in my closet. Almost every night he would come to visit me while I tried to sleep. At first, I tried to pile stuffed animals on one side of the bed and hide behind them—thinking I had outsmarted the little boy—but he would only peek over the top, and look down on me.

He had third degree burns on most of his body, and the sight of him would send me screaming until I was hoarse.

Soon after seeing him for the first time, my night terrors began. I learned to stay awake as long as possible, but sleep would overtake me in the small hours of the morning, sending me into dreams of fire. In some dreams, my room would be ablaze and I would be trapped. In others, I would find myself in the burn unit of some hospital in terrible pain and dying. In one, a shadow figure came into my room, doused me in gasoline and set me afire. My screams would wake my parents and they would find me drenched in sweat, shaking and exhausted.

I developed a phobia of fire that caused me to check the heater and oven compulsively for defects, and to cry whenever my mother would light a match to burn a candle or work the gas stove. They tried to help by installing smoke detectors in every room, and allowing me to sleep with a fire extinguisher, but it wasn't enough. To keep the entities at bay, my father finally resorted to circling my bed with crosses telling me that whatever was in the house would have no power with me so protected. That seemed to work for a little while, but the activity came back, and as such the crosses were abandoned.

Leta and her father on her 10th birthday, in the driveway of the GI house.

One night when I was ten, I was sitting up in bed reading. I looked at my clock and saw that it was 4 AM. The house had been quiet thus far, and as I had school the next morning, I felt it was finally safe to catch a couple desperate hours of sleep. I placed my book on the nightstand and was just about to turn off my lamp, when something compelled me to look up at my doorway. There stood my mother dressed in her favorite jeans, flannel shirt and white Reeboks. She glared at me sternly and shouted, "Don't put that there!"

I looked at her confused. Did she mean my book? The lamp? I started to ask what she meant and why she wasn't in pajamas, when I realized that I could clearly see the clothes hamper through her. She faded slowly away, and I spent the rest of the early morning too terrified to sleep.

When the clock alarm finally went off, I made my way to the bathroom. I stopped when I came to my parents' room and saw that mom was also getting out of bed to make breakfast. I was mulling over whether I should tell her about my strange visitor, when I glanced over and noticed that her favorite jeans and flannel shirt were hanging on the doorknob of her door. I almost became sick as I stared at the clothing the entity had seen and emulated. The image burned itself in my brain. Mom in her pajamas getting out of bed, and those clothes hanging there while my stomach churned and tears stung my eyes. It was one thing to see shadow figures, but for an entity to take the image of a loved one, made me fear it all the more.

Leta at age six, in front of the TV that turned on at night.

At fourteen, we moved into a new house in Tennessee, and I was finally free of the evil that lived in that old GI house.

When I got older, my father finally admitted that when I was just a baby, he had placed a tape recorder on the kitchen table and told spirits to speak into it. The next morning, they heard an angry male voice but couldn't make out the words. It scared my mother so much she ripped the tape out of the cassette, and threw it in the garbage. It was shortly afterward that a small man would visit dad at night, and dad would hear the sounds of a party in the living room—clinking glasses, shuffling feet, and several conversations going on at once. The small man would come to the door of the bedroom, and wave to my dad saying, "Come on, Ray. Come to the party with us!" He would continue until dad would start to get out of bed, and suddenly the sounds and the small man would disappear. This plagued him for years.

We were also able to finally talk about the TV. It was the old style that had to "warm up" and gave off the sound of static electricity when you turned it on. Almost every night we would hear it turn on, and then hear someone or something using the remote to quickly click through all the channels, over and over again. One of us would get out of bed and start walking toward the living room, at which time the TV would turn itself off—just before we walked into the room. We both knew we were "taking turns" as it were to stop the TV, but were too afraid to acknowledge it while living there.

I'm now 36, married and living in a quiet and peaceful house in Tennessee. Occasionally, I still have sightings of ghosts, or will have a strange occurrence of foreknowledge that always comes true. They're never scary, though. But even after all these years, that GI house haunts me sometimes. I still have trouble falling asleep after dark, and the thought of fire always fills me with an unspeakably deep dread.

Anything Ghost Show, Episode #238

The Leaping Shadow Person
William (Utah, U.S.)

About ten years ago I was living with my parents. Their house is nothing special—I think one family lived in it for a few months after it was built, but had to move away due to changing jobs. So basically, my parents were the first people to really settle in it. They've lived there for about 40 years. I wouldn't say the house is haunted, but I do believe the land may be.

We've all experienced some strange things in and around the house. My brother teases that it's my fault because I've also been told that my aura is pretty and attracts spirits. One night, I stayed up late reading Voyager in the Outlander series—so it wasn't even a spooky book! At about 11:30 PM, I decided it was time to go to sleep, so I got out of bed and walked down the hall to get a glass of milk. Instead of turning left into the kitchen, I walked into the living room (which was adjacent to the kitchen and dining room). It was a cold rainy night, and I had an old beagle (named Snoopy) who would chill easily, so I covered him with his blanket. He sighed and stretched a bit, snuggling into the blanket.

I crossed back through the room and into the kitchen, poured some milk, and as I walked back to the hallway, I glanced out into the living room again. The big window on the other side of the room had wooden blinds that my parents kept cracked open at night (allowing light from the streetlamp to come shining in). When I looked over, I saw a figure blocking out some of the window. It had been moving, as I was, but it seemed we both stopped at the same time—like deer in headlights. The kitchen had a very dim nightlight that shined just into the living room, and it was then that I realized the true horror: the figure was NOT outside on the porch...it was in the living room!

It stood close to my dog on his bed, separating us. It was about six feet tall, with a sort of stocky build. I could somewhat see through it, but it distorted the view slightly, like when looking through water or old glass. It was also three-dimensional: the fatter parts like the center of arms and legs were much darker than the edges. I was breathing fast and heavy in terror, and it felt like my heart was going to pound out of my chest.

My dog must have seen or sensed my fear, and I heard him growl a very low, quiet, but serious growl. The shadow figure then looked back at my dog, then back towards me, and then immediately jumped head and hands first into the dark shadow behind a chair; and like a diver off a diving board, or a gymnast performing a flip, its whole body followed slowly—sort of stretching the figure out, but following the curve of the jump like a black rainbow across the room.

I immediately ran down the hall to my bedroom, and hid under the covers.

I eventually fell asleep, and when I woke the next morning, the door that I had left open, only because fear wanted me to hide as soon as possible, was closed. I asked everyone in my family, but they all denied closing it.

As I said earlier, I've seen shadow people, but like most people, they've been further away, or just a glimpse. That was the first time I'd ever seen one so close, and long enough to study it. Since then, I've sort of become accustomed to them; and although they still startle and scare me, I think of them as a spider on the wall—especially since that one seemed just as afraid of me as I was of it.

I see them sometimes for many consecutive days at a time, and then they go away for a while.

Anything Ghost Show, Episode #230

House Sitting
Carla (Winston Salem, North Carolina)

The following story happened to a friend of mine just recently. First let me describe him because it is relevant. His name is Charles, and he is a 43-year-old high school teacher—and is very much an intellectual. He is always logical about everything, and is very serious. To believe in paranormal phenomena is a great big stretch for him. He feels that a lot of events just happen because over blown imagination. I am more open-minded and we often get into arguments about the subject. But he is a manly man. You know, the type that loves his bike and carries a gun wherever he goes. He is not afraid to deal with you, if he has to.

A couple of months ago he was in the transition of moving into a new home. He was caught in between a rock and a hard place because the house he was moving into was not ready, and he had to move out of the house he was in. His friend was going to be out of town for a while and he offered him to stay in his house while he was away. So my friend took him up on it.

The first few nights were pleasant and uneventful. But late one evening he walked into the house and felt a little uneasy. You how it feels when you come into a room and you can just feel that someone was there or had just left? Well of course, he got his gun out and he went all over the house, but found nothing disturbed and no one present. So he figured it was his imagination.

It's difficult to describe the house, except to say that it had two stories with an addition. The addition to the house is a guest bedroom and study that was positioned to where the stairs that went up stairs had a landing half way up. The door to the addition was open to that landing then the stairs continued up to the second floor. In other words, if you were in that guest room looking out the door you could see who ever would be coming down those stairs.

The following is creeping me out just typing it for you...

After checking the house and securing everything, Charles went into the guest room to settle in and watch some TV. While he was sitting there he heard movement up stairs. He didn't investigate right away he just turned the TV down to listen. He soon heard the movement start going down the stairs. He thought to himself about getting the gun, but it was across the room from him and he still wasn't sure what he was hearing. As he sat there and heard the steps creek from up stairs down closer to the landing, he looked at the door: it was still open to the stairs. As he was looking, he saw a man walk right past the door. As the man walked past, he turned his head and looked at him (without any surprise or care), and continued down the steps. Charles said that the man looked like an Indian, and was carrying something in his hands that looked like a covered tray.

Of course Charles thought someone had broken in and he sprang up and got his gun and ran to the stairwell to confront the man but when he got to the door and looked down the stairs no one was there. He said he went all the way to the bottom and looked all over the ground floor—and there just wasn't anyone there. He was truly shaken by this, and went to stay in a hotel with money he really didn't have to spare.

You have to know him like I do to appreciate the story. He is the type that is not afraid of anything, and has an explanation for everything...except that experience.

He called his friend and told him what had happened. His friend said he has never experienced anything in that house before. He did know that the house was located near an old reservation, but that was it.

I think that Charles was extra sensitive, and was just at the right place at the right time to see what he did.

Trust me when I say: we don't argue about the unknown as much since that experience.

Anything Ghost Show, Episode #67

The Unwelcome Visitor
Chris (Nashville, Tennessee)

When I was in high school, I had a friend named Cassie who insisted her house was haunted. Back then, I was a bit of a skeptic who wasn't sure what to believe about the paranormal, so she invited me to spend a night at her place. It was during the summer, and she guaranteed that I would become a believer.

After I arrived at her house, Cassie's mother explained a little bit about the history of the home, and the spirit she thought was haunting it.

The house was built in the late 70's by an architect in town; it was built to be a retirement estate for him and his wife. Unfortunately, he passed away shortly after it's completion. His wife, however, lived to be a very old woman and became a recluse after his death. She lived in the house until the late 80's and apparently had been dead for a while before anyone found her body.

Cassie's mom insisted this woman's spirit was still trapped in the house, and regularly disturbed objects and people in the home. Regularly, her and her husband would wake up to the bed vibrating as if someone was shaking it or kicking it. Sometimes she would feel the bed move, as if someone sat down on it—but no one would be there (this even happened during the day). They also and an issue with guests complaining about strange noises at night like footsteps, as well as lights turning on and off. She also said the spirit seemed to dislike men more than women.

Thinking Cassie was up to a prank, I assumed Cassie's mom was in on the joke, and did not take it seriously.

When I was ready for bed, I made sure to lock my door to ensure no one would try to mess with me while I slept. If there was anything paranormal going on in the house, I wanted to make sure it was real.

That summer I had an internship with a local company and needed to be up early in the morning. So I set an alarm on my phone before going to bed. I distinctly remember putting my phone on the night stand next to the bed before turning the lights off.

Everything was quiet during the night, until a loud clatter coming from the bathroom woke me up. I didn't see anything, so I assumed it was the air condition clicking on, and thought no more about it.

The rest of the night passed without any further disturbance.

I woke up in the morning, three hours late for work. My phone was missing from the nightstand, and I frantically tried to find it so I could get out the door. I searched everywhere in the bedroom, but to no avail.

I ended up finding it in the bathroom, on the floor, face down and turned off. I can't explain how it got there and can't explain why it was there; but I remembered the noise that I heard in the night, and I assumed the two things had to be connected. I dismissed this too as some kind of practical joke my friend was playing and went to work. To this day, she insists she did not move my phone that night.

A couple years went by before I had another opportunity to stay at Cassie's house. There were many of us gathered there for her birthday party, and I offered to sleep on an inflatable mattress in the bonus room (so the girls could have all the bedrooms).

The bonus room was situated in such a way that the inflatable mattress was in the middle of the room, with site-lines to the long hallway that stretched from one side of the house to the other. There was no way for anyone to get into the room without me seeing them come down the hall. There were no other entrances to the room.

I remember having very troubled dreams that night and did not sleep well. As I drifted in and out of sleep, I became acutely aware of a noise from the far end of the hall. While I couldn't see all the way down the hall (as it was completely black and I didn't have my glasses on), I remember a feeling of complete dread washing over me each time I looked down the hall.

Later, I awoke to the sound of footsteps coming towards me. They were not loud, but they were decidedly audible in the otherwise silent house. I opened my eyes to see who it was, but no one was there. The steps, however, kept coming and were getting louder and louder as they came down the hall! Not knowing what to do, I stayed frozen in place—hoping whatever it was wouldn't see me and would leave me alone. Eventually, the footsteps stopped coming towards me, and the house fell silent again. I lied there listening intently for any sign of movement, but there was nothing.

I waited a few minutes before I tried to get back to sleep, but the hairs on the back of my neck were erect like porcupine needles.

I must have fallen asleep for a little bit, because I woke up suddenly (and very cold), and I heard shallow breathing right above my ear. It didn't sound at all natural: it sounded as if it was coming from under water. I closed my eyes as tight as I could, terrified.

Then, a dry voice said in a harsh whisper, "Get up." The voice was unmistakably a woman's.

I vomited on the spot as a wave of nausea hit me, and I ran out of the room as quickly as I could—not daring to look back.

I stayed in that house only one more time—and certainly not by choice. And while my experience this last time was not as bad as the previous, it was still creepy: the lights in the guest room turned on and off randomly; and the door (which I always locked) would be open every time I woke up.

I recently found out Cassie's mother had had enough of whatever spirit was in their home, and went through the necessary measures to cleanse it. They have not had further disturbances; but even though everything has settled down, I've made it clear to Cassie I would never stay at her house again, because I felt like an unwelcome visitor.

Anything Ghost Show, Episode #227

Oregon Ghost Stories
Savanna (Oregon, U.S.)

This experience happened when I was about seven, and I was staying with my grandparents on their farm. It was night, and I had a cold. Just a regular cold, not something that would cause hallucinations or anything. I was lying in bed, and looking out the bedroom door into the dark hall. Everyone was in bed at that point. Out of nowhere, I saw an old woman standing just outside the door. She wasn't scary and I didn't have a bad feeling seeing her. She looked like someone's grandmother. She was wearing an older style dress with a white apron and she was holding a tray (with what looked like a bottle of medicine and a big spoon). She was smiling at me, and she started to slowly come towards me. But she wasn't walking, she was slowly gliding (all the while smiling at me). I still got scared though, and pulled the blanket over my head.

I waited for a few seconds, and slowly lowered the blanket.

She was gone.

I told my mom about it, and she told me she thought it was my great grandmother (she had died a few months before that). I didn't know her well, so I can't be sure.

When I was about nine years old, we moved into a new house, and slowly but surely some weird sounds and occurrences began to happen. It was a three bedroom, one bathhouse that was built in the 1960's.

First, my mom and I would regularly hear a baby crying. I'd say, "Hey mom! Do you hear that?"

She would reply, "You mean the baby crying? Yep! I don't know where it's coming from, though!"

It always sounded like it was coming from the bedrooms, but then we would get down the hall, and the crying would drift away. We asked around the neighborhood if anyone had a new baby, but there were no babies at all.

One time there was a cable man setting us up with cable, and he told my mom, "Hey, I think your baby is crying!"

Mom said, "We don't have a baby—but we do have a ghost baby!"

He turned white, finished the job as quickly as possible, and took off!

We would also regularly hear what sounded like a toddler, running back and forth in the attic: little feet, thumping back and forth, at all hours of the day.

There was another weird thing that would happen: whenever went somewhere and left puzzles or model car materials on the kitchen table, when we got back, everything would be put away into the craft closet. It happened all the time! We would just joke about how we had a friendly "maid" ghost.

Finally, we would regularly hear my little brother (who was about three at the time), talking to himself in his bedroom. Well, not really talking to himself so much as having a conversation. He told us it was a child that was his age.

When we moved into the last house my mom bought, I was about thirteen years old. It was obvious pretty quickly that there was a presence there. One of them was always in my room. It didn't make itself known very often, but it was definitely there. Every couple of months I would awake, look up at the ceiling, and see a face there—a white face with crooked, pointed teeth, and dark circles around the eyes. No hair, just the face. It would stare down at me; kind of hovering in circles. I would always close my eyes a few times, and try to get the face to go away; but it would hang out for about thirty minutes, and then it would slowly disappear.

Last year during Christmas, my family and I were talking about the various things we'd seen in the house. After I had moved out, my brother moved into my bedroom. During our discussion, he told me the very same story about the white face above his bed on the ceiling. I looked at him, shocked; I had never told anyone about that before; so it was very validating to hear that he went through the same thing.

Another thing that everyone in my family saw was a large shadow man. He was very tall—about seven feet! He hung out in the hallway, in a little nook by the front door. He also liked to stand in my mom's bedroom, and look down at her when she slept. She has woken up multiple times to this entity staring down at her, thinking it was my dad. She would yell, "Hey! What are you doing!"

Then she would realize that my dad was asleep next to her. She would yell again for it to "go away," "I don't want you in here," and they would entity disappear.

Now that my brothers and I are grown and have children of our own, they sleep in my old room when they stay at my mom's. Luckily, they haven't seen anything yet. But that may be because my mom cleansed the house with sage about six months ago. She walked around the house with all the windows and doors open, telling the spirits that it was time for them to go, and that she didn't want them scaring the children.

No one has seen anything since.

Anything Ghost Show, Episode #228

Something was in Our Townhouse
Amberly (Topeka, Kansas)

Two years ago my husband Caleb and our three children (Austyn was six, Evan was five, and Jaxon was one) all lived in a two-bedroom townhouse. Within a few months of us living there, our oldest child Austyn, started to suffer from night terrors (which she'd never had before); it was very disturbing, but she never remembered them the next day. After researching night terrors, we knew there was nothing we could really do but ignore them, and hope she would grow out of them.

"...our oldest child Austyn started to suffer from night terrors."

However, things started to get even more weird: objects like keys and cell-phones, would seem to just fall off end tables and counters by themselves (my husband would always reassure me that it was nothing, and that we were just setting things to close to the edge—but I knew that wasn't the case); TV's would turn on and off by themselves; and one night we even heard what sounded like people whispering in our children's bedrooms—and when my husband went into their room to tell them to be quiet and go to bed, they were already asleep; and friends didn't want to sleep at our place because they thought they heard things in our basement.

"...they thought they heard things in our basement."

Even with all this, my husband refused to believe anything paranormal was going on. However, that wouldn't last much longer: after months of little things happening, us ignoring them—acting like nothing out of the ordinary was happening—we had two very scary nights.

The first night, we all had stayed up late in the living room watching movies. Myself, Austyn and our youngest child Jaxon went upstairs to go to sleep; that left my husband and middle child, Evan, to sleep in the living room.

My husband woke up in the middle of the night and saw a shadow walking up the stairs. Thinking it was Evan, he sat up and said, "Evan what are you doing?"

"Evan where are you going?"

Evan sat up behind my husband sleepy and confused asking, "What daddy?"

That shadow walking up the stairs was not our son! My husband immediately got chills but tried to tell himself that he was just seeing things. He didn't tell me this story right away for fear of scaring me.

Two nights after that happened, my daughter Austyn was sleeping on my bedroom floor and I was sleeping in my bed. I woke up in the middle of the night and saw a shadow figure crouched down next to her. Thinking it was my husband, I said, "Caleb? What are you doing?"

The shadow figure turned its head towards me, and disappeared right in front of my eyes. I screamed, jumped out of bed and turned the light on.

All the commotion woke my husband up, and I told him right away what I had seen; that's when he told me about his experience from two days earlier.

The shadow man visits were the breaking point for us. We had planned on buying a house eventually (because we needed more space); however, this made us jump-start the process, and within a few months we were in our new home.

After moving into our new home things were peaceful: we didn't hear anymore voices; things didn't fall off counters; and the biggest change of all was that my daughter's night terrors stopped instantly.

We have moved on from that townhouse but what happened there still haunts my family and we still talk about it from time to time. I'm not sure what was in that townhouse but whatever it is I'm glad it stayed there and didn't follow us to our new home.

Anything Ghost Show, Episode #238

Grandpa's Ghost
Tara (Alberta, Canada)

I went to high school in Illinois, and was friends with a girl named Rae. We generally had a group of three to six kids who would all hang out at Rae's house after school. Being there so often, I often noticed that one of the cupboards in the kitchen was never fully closed. It was always just open enough to put your hand in, and take out a cup. Even if you fully closed it, you'd find it open again a little while later. I figured it just didn't close properly, and ignored it mostly.

I spent the night at her house twice. The first time I spent the night, Rae told me not to be worried if I heard anything from the kitchen during the night (the cupboard tends to open and hit the other cupboard next to it). She never gave any real reason. Then again, I hadn't asked either.

I woke up somewhere around 4 AM needing to use the restroom. Rae's room was at the end of a short hall of which her mother's bedroom door was right outside, and the bathroom was right next to that. The hall opened into the living room with the kitchen just off to the left next to the bathroom. I carefully, and quietly left the bedroom as not to disturb Rae or our other friend's sleep. The first thing I noticed when I left the bedroom was the drastic change in temperature. It had been quite warm in the bedroom, but the hallway was freezing. I quickly went into the bathroom so I could get back to the warm blanket as soon as possible.

After exiting the bathroom, I heard a "thunk" from the kitchen. I took a quick peek into the living room and kitchen, just in case. The cupboard was slightly open as it always was, but there wasn't anyone there. I got the sudden feeling that I shouldn't be there—it felt like someone was staring at me. I knew if I stayed there too long, I'd freak myself out and never get back to sleep. So, down the hall to the bedroom I started.

Whack!

The sudden, loud noise made me jump and spin around towards the living room once more. I took another look into the kitchen. There was no way there wasn't someone or something in there.

Nothing.

Nothing but that cupboard, which was now fully open.

I went straight back to the bedroom, closed the door, and laid there sleeplessly for a while. I debated for some time bringing up what happened, and decided to keep it to myself for the time being.

The second time I spent the night there was a few weeks later for Rae's birthday. There were four girls were sitting around, watching TV in the living room late at night. After our show was over, we were still wide awake (despite it being 3 AM). One girl suggested we tell scary stories.

After a cheesy ghost story was told, Rae spoke up. "My grandpa still lives here," she started. "He hangs out in the kitchen and living room at night. So, if you ever hear any odd noises at night, I wouldn't worry about it."

I asked her what she meant. She pointed into the kitchen, at the cupboards that were all closed at the time.

"The cupboard we keep glasses in gets opened all the time. Sometimes we'll find a clean glass just sitting on the counter, too. It's always the same glass. It was his favorite, I guess."

Remembering my experience from sleeping over previously, I told her about it. It was much too coincidental for me.

Rae just laughed, and said, "Yeah, I've had some complaints about him being mean at night. I don't know why. I probably should have given you more warning. Sorry about that."

Our other two friends just scoffed at the story. They very much didn't believe it, and I didn't blame them. They accused us of just making up the story together to scare them.

While trying to convince them we weren't making anything up, a birthday card on the table moved. I don't mean it moved a little bit either. It flipped itself up and over a small box. The card landed upright, leaning against a stack of coasters. It was as if someone picked it up, and quickly placed it there. No one had been close enough to physically move the card.

One girl picked up the card, as if looking for strings or something.

"Did you see that?"

"How did that flip like that?"

Rae just laughed at us. "I told you: my grandpa hangs out in here. Hi grandpa!"

We never spoke of it again.

Anything Ghost Show, Episode #225

The Lady in Black

Nathan (New Bethlehem, Pennsylvania)

This experience happened to my three sisters and myself in 1971 in our hometown of Clearfield, Pennsylvania.

I was nine years old when this story took place, but I remember it like it was yesterday. I am the youngest, and only boy, of five children.

In 1971, our parents bought a huge old house on South Second Street. The house had two marble fireplaces, beautiful woodwork, hardwood floors, and stained glass windows. It had been neglected, but was still in good condition, and they got it at a good price. So, we moved and began fixing it up little by little. The house ended up being the family home for over forty years. But these events took place the first few months that we lived there. At the time, I was in the second grade, and living there with my parents and my three older sisters.

Our parents' bedroom was on the first floor, while all of the kids had bedrooms on the second floor. After going up the huge staircase, a long L-shaped corridor led to each bedroom. My room was first; then Linda, Debbie and Bonnie's; and the last room at the end of the long hall was the bathroom.

Mom and dad would get up much earlier than the rest of us to go to work. That left the older girls to make sure the younger ones were up and ready for school.

I must point out now that these events could be easily explained away by the power of suggestion (as in one person telling another person); however, that was not the case: as NOT one of the four of us had shared any personal experiences with each, other until after the fact—which is what made us believe we really had been haunted.

Nathan's childhood home in Clearfield, Pennsylvania.

It begins:

One night, our oldest sister Bonnie was lying in her bed reading. After a time, she began to have an "uneasy" feeling. Upon looking up from her book, she was startled to see a lady leaning into the doorway of her bedroom. The lady was looking in at her. She had dark hair swept up in a high "Gibson Girl" hairstyle, and a long skirt black dress with a high collar with long sleeves and puffed shoulders. My sister said the lady stared at her rather unkindly—to the extent that she felt a little frightened. My sister got hold of her courage, and firmly told the lady to "Go away!"

She then closed her eyes and opened them again...the lady in black had gone.

She did not sleep well that night, but eventually things went back to normal for her, and she quickly forgot about it—reasoning, that her eyes were tired from reading too much.

On a morning not long after this, Bonnie (who had seen the lady in black) woke our sister Debbie for school. Debbie made her way down the hall to go into the bathroom, but realized that Bonnie was not out of the bathroom yet. So rather than walk back down the hall to her room, she went to lay down on Bonnie's bed to wait.

She had not been resting long, when she had a strange feeling and opened her eyes. There, she saw a lady in a long black dress with dark hair leaning over the bed staring at her with an unkind look. For a second, Debbie thought it was Bonnie scolding her for falling back asleep when she should get ready for school!

Debbie said, "I'm awake! I'm getting up!"

The lady disappeared.

"What did you say?" Bonnie responded from the bathroom.

That made Debbie realize it truly was NOT Bonnie standing in the room.

On another occasion, my sister Linda came home from work for lunch. She started to go upstairs to get something, but stopped halfway up. Standing at the top of the stairs, and looking down, was the lady in black. It frightened Linda so much that she spun around, hurried back down the stairs and out of the house. She said as she sat in the car in the driveway after that; she looked up at the window at the top of the stairs, and saw a dark silhouetted figure watching her.

Lastly.

I was getting dressed one morning, and Linda was going to take me to school. She had warned me to hurry (as she didn't want to be late for work). I put on my pants and shirt, grabbed my shoes and socks, and raced downstairs—thinking I would beat her to the kitchen and be waiting when she came down. I was sitting in the chair putting on my socks, when I had a strange feeling. I looked over to see the lady dressed in black—her dark hair pinned up—she was leaning in the doorway watching me. I thought it was my sister Linda making sure I was getting ready, so I continued to tie my shoes. But when I looked up again the lady was gone.

Thinking nothing of it, I proceeded into the kitchen where I was surprised to see Linda—and her hair was NOT pinned up as I had just seen her. I asked her how she got her hair brushed out and got downstairs so quickly. She looked at me strangely and said it she had been downstairs for quite a while.

Other odd things happened:

- Lights would go on and off.
- When we were downstairs we would sometimes hear walking on the floor above—when nobody was upstairs.

But after we had lived there about a year, it became home, and nothing strange ever happened again. The four the siblings never mentioned these incidents to each other until about seven years later.

"...looked behind the fireplace and found two pieces of mail..."

After the ghostly activity came to an end, the beautiful old marble fireplace began to come loose from the wall, and my dad set out to repair it. Before putting it back in place, my dad looked behind the fireplace and found two pieces of mail: a birthday greeting card, and a post card of "congratulations on the new house." Both of these were written to Mrs. L.C. Norris, and were addressed to our home. The stamped post date was 1908.

When he pulled the fireplace out a little further, my dad noticed something else: he reached in and pulled out an old, faded photograph. The photo was of a lady in a long black dress with a high collar with long sleeves and puffed shoulders. Her hair was piled into a Gibson Girl hair style, and she wore a large hat with a feather plum in it.

"When he pulled the fireplace out a little further, my dad noticed something else..."

The four of us looked at the old photograph, and immediately recognized our Lady in Black (from seeing her the first year we lived there).

That was when we began to share our individual experiences with each other.

We decided that the lady in black was just checking us out to see what kind of people were living in her house. Once she saw we meant no harm, and were fixing it up, she stopped coming.

We never did see her again; but from then on, as we grew up, we would re-tell how when we first moved into the house, and how we had each been visited by "the Lady in Black."

Anything Ghost Show, Episode #237

Shadows of Feet Under the Door
Marcy (Dallas, Texas)

I grew up in an old church parsonage in a small Minnesota town. The house was close to 100 years old.

One weekend, when I was sixteen, I was at home alone. The day progressed without anything unusual happening. I went to bed, I forget what time, but fell asleep without incident. At exactly 2:11 AM, I awoke suddenly. I felt scared for some reason, and stayed still in bed silently listening for whatever had awakened me. Because our house was so old, there were many noises it made when certain things happened—and I had memorized them all as a teenager (who liked to sneak out and avoid making those noises). For instance, when an exterior door was opened or closed downstairs, all of the bedroom doors upstairs would rattle slightly from the change in air pressure; and there were certain steps on the stairs leading up to the bedrooms that would creak when stepped on.

At first, I heard nothing when I woke up. But then something happened that made my blood run cold: I heard the door to our garage downstairs slam shut. It was metal and hollow cored and was very distinct, so there was no mistaking the sound as something else. I had locked that door before I went to bed—and of course, because a door closed downstairs, my bedroom door upstairs rattled immediately afterward. I thought it may have been my imagination—or perhaps part of a dream sticking with me—so I tried to calm myself, but continued to listen intently.

Not long after the door slammed, I heard someone slowly walking up the stairs leading to my bedroom. Each step that would always creak when pressure was placed on it, did so. Now I was terrified. Someone had broken into the house! This was back before the days of cell phones, so I had no way to call for help. I began to think about how I could hide or escape—but my room was at the very top of the stairs, and there was no way.

In the hallway my mom kept a night light burning (and let me reiterate that because the house was so old, there were big gaps at the bottom of all the bedroom doors), so I was able to see the night light shining underneath. As the intruder got to the top of the stairs, everything went quiet again; and by that time I had put my head under my covers, and was trying not to breathe loudly—hoping whoever it was wouldn't hear me.

I didn't hear another sound for several minutes, and I finally made myself come out from under the covers, and look over at my door. From underneath, I saw the shadows of two feet standing directly outside my bedroom—blocking the light from the night light. My eyes went wide and my mouth went dry. I dove back under the covers—crying now. I was a dead girl for sure.

I waited for what seemed like an eternity, but who knows exactly how long it actually was.

No other noises were made.

I ventured a peak over at the door again, just one eyeball from under my blanket.

Nothing.

The shadow feet were gone. There was only the full glow of the night-light. How did I miss the person walking away?

Again, I waited for what seemed like forever, and finally I decided that I would rather get up and confront whoever this was rather than wait all night for him to kill me. I have no idea where that sixteen-year-old girl got the bravery to do this, but I got out of bed and threw my bedroom door open.

Nothing in the hallway.

All the other doors were closed (as I had left them when I went to bed). One by one, I crept into each room: checking closets and under beds. Nobody was there. I quietly walked downstairs (now armed with a plunger from the bathroom as my weapon). I couldn't find anything out of place, or a strange person—anywhere downstairs, either. Lastly, I checked the garage door and front door. Both were locked from the inside.

I was alone.

I never found out what or who those shadow feet belonged to. Many times after that night, I would feel as if someone was watching me or following me in the house. I began to talk out loud and tell whatever it was that it was okay for them to be in the house, but please don't scare me again. I never had another experience quite like that one.

A couple years later, a boyfriend I had at the time, revealed to me that one night when he slept over with me in that house; he woke up at 2:11 AM and saw the shadows of feet under my door. He thought he was just seeing things, so he rolled over, went back to sleep and didn't tell me.

Anything Ghost Show, Episode #248

Chapter Seven

Outdoors

These perturbations, this perpetual jar
Of earthly wants and aspirations high,
Come from the influence of an unseen star
An undiscovered planet in our sky.

(Poem Continues in Chapter 8.)

The Fire of 1910
Paul (Los Angeles, California)

This story takes place in northern Minnesota on October 7th in the early 1980's. My parents had a large farm out in the woods. We were very secluded out there, however, once in a while they would go into town to go shopping...and this was one of those days.

They had been gone all day when they surprised us with a phone call. They asked me and my older brother to meet them at a small restaurant about fifteen miles away. Excited to get off the farm for a while, we hopped into my brother's car and headed down the gravel back-roads.

We decided to go a specific way to the restaurant: one that would take us by a particular road that lead down to a county landfill (black bears were often seen there). On the approach to this road, there was a large forty acre field on our left that the farmer had been trying to clear of trees for many years (it was nearly completed).

As we approached the field, the farmer just happened to be burning one of the last piles of wood. The flames were large and he was tossing more wood on to the top. My brother and I commented that it was nice to see he was nearly done clearing the field.

We came up to the intersection of the landfill road, stopped, and looked down the road to our right—hoping to see a black bear (of which there were none). Mildly disappointed, we turned left along the other edge of the field. Our attention went back to the large fire again. However, this time there was nothing out there.

My brother turned to me and said, "Um. Wasn't there just a guy out there burning stuff?"

I responded, "Yes."

We stopped the car, and looked over the entire field—we even walked out there when we realized the whole field was full of dead, dry grass. Any flames, and the whole thing would have been on fire.

Soon after that day and that incident, I happened across some local history telling of a large fire that tore through that area on October 7, 1910. The fire killed 29 to 42 people. What's more astonishing is that twelve people died right near that spot—they jumped into a well to escape the flames and suffocated.

I don't know if what we saw was related. But I can still see the farmer in overalls tossing sticks on to a large fire. My brother and I often recount the vision we both saw that day.

Anything Ghost Show, Episode #245

The Field
Alan (California, U.S.)

This story took place in central California in mid-1980.

I grew up down the street from my good buddy Steve, who to this day is still my closest friend.

Directly across the street from Steve's house was vacant lot. We didn't think it was strange back then; but now it seems peculiar that a well-established, older neighborhood with fully-grown trees and families, had a vacant lot right in the center. But it was there—and my friend and I loved it! We named it, "the Field." That's where we'd play every afternoon; and each Saturday morning, Steve and I would go out to the field with our army clothes and our toy guns—we would build forts and dig holes. That was OUR spot.

Most of the other kids in the neighborhood were older than us, and they never went near the field. They all referred to it as, "the Haunted Field."

Steve's bedroom window had a clear view of the field, and he said he never saw anyone out there—except on occasion, he'd see a little blond kid running around in the field. But neither of us knew him, and the little kid didn't mess with our fort or any of our stuff. We pretty much had the field all to ourselves.

There was a large pile of wood scraps and rubble in the corner of the field that Steve's dad warned us not to play in—he warned us many times that there were rusty nails, black widows and all sorts of things in there, and to "stay away from it!"

We did stay away from that woodpile, but not because of what Steve's dad warned us about. We stayed away because of what the neighborhood kids said: "That was where the ghost lived."

The story was that if you went out to the woodpile just before sunrise, you would see the ghost climb out and hop on its one leg down the street. That terrified us! So we stayed away from the pile of rubble—in fact, we stayed away from that side of the field.

One Saturday morning, as usual, I put on my army clothes, gathered up my toy guns and walked over to the field. When I got to there, Steve began telling me that he had talked to the little blond kid earlier that morning. The kid told Steve that a house was going to be built in the field soon; and that his dad drove the bobcat tractor for the construction company that was going to be building the house.

The idea of our field being used for a new home was devastating to the both of us. We started counting down the days until we would no longer have our field.

Steve told his parents what the kid had told him about the new home being built; and his dad suggested that we go in there and make sure to remove all our toys (before the construction company began its work). We did, and we were sad to do it. But the day came when we finally had all of our stuff removed, and said our last good-bye to the field.

A week went by, and there were no signs of construction.

Another week went by, and still nothing.

At that point, I suggested to Steve that we grab all our stuff and start playing in the field again. But Steve told me that he saw the little blond kid again, and the told him the same thing again. He said his dad and the crew will be out there the next day to start building the house.

Weeks went by and still nothing.

Months went by.

Years went by.

Illustration of the woodpile ghost by Alan

Steve and I grew older and began middle school, and that field became a part of our past.

By the time I was a senior in high school, I drove by the field and noticed a construction crew. So I got out of my car. I was feeling a little nostalgic, and I was walking around the field for one last look. I began talking to one of the construction workers, and was telling him how I used to play out there—I pointed out areas of where our forts were, and whatnot.

I eventually asked him, "Don't you think it's strange that for all these years, in a neighborhood like this, there would be an empty lot sitting here?"

He told me that the reason a house was never built here was because of the tragedy that happened 25 or 30 years ago.

I will never forget the cold chills that ran through my body when he said that—I have those chills right now as I reflect on that moment.

The construction man told me that a house was being built on that lot—when the neighborhood was new. A little boy used to come to work with his father at the site. On one of those days there was an accident in which the little boy lost his leg, and unfortunately he bled to death in the field.

Construction was put to a halt, and all the building materials were piled up in the corner of the field.

Nobody ever came back to our field.

Anything Ghost Show, Episode #245

Forest Spirits
Nissim (New Delhi, India)

This is the story of my first experience with a paranormal entity. My great-aunt calls them "forest spirits".

India has a diverse culture and different groups of people have their own lifestyles. I come from a tribal community who dwell in villages near and in forests. Though my family lives in a big city, some of my distant relatives still live in a village far away.

It was in the year 1999, I was 6 years old, and enjoying my summer vacation. A couple of my aunts decided to pay their aunt a visit who lived in the village. Since I'd never been there, I asked them to take me along with them.

The following weekend, we took a train, then a bus. As we were reaching closer to our destination, I noticed there were less and less buildings, no roads, and no utility poles. There was no power supply where we were going, so it was going to be really dark at night.

It was in the late afternoon when we reached my great-aunty's home.

She lived alone. Her husband had passed away few years prior. Her house was towards the outer parts of the village that was slightly close to the forest, but behind the community church—so it used to get a rather bustling after church services.

The community church near Nissim's great-aunt's house (in India).

It got quite dark as we settled into the house. The only source of light was the wood fire in the garden where dinner was being prepared. Bored, I went into the house and lied down on the bed. A little light was entering through the window above the bed, but other than that it was way darker when compared to a power outage in cities.

Nissim's great-aunt's house (India).

I stared into the darkness thinking about the next day. Suddenly, someone touched my head. Someone's hand was gently rubbing my head, and sometimes patting it. Curious, I got up in an instant and groped about in the darkness. I thought perhaps it was my great-aunt, but I couldn't find anyone there. I looked through the window and saw she was far away in the garden, cooking. Both my aunts were there too!

I ran outside towards them and I explained everything that had happened. I was very curious, as nothing like that had ever happened to me. My great-aunty told us that it was a spirit that lives in the forest who wanders in the village, touching people. She said that almost every one in the village has been visited by this particular spirit, but it never caused anyone trouble. She went on to tell me about all the other spirits who live in the forest.

I felt I was lucky to have not been visited by the one who "sucks her victim's blood while they're asleep."

That was the first time I'd ever felt so scared of anything. Also, I had a really bad fever that night. Great aunty said that the spirit who touched me did it.

I was okay by morning.

Anything Ghost Show, Episode #231

The Little Yellow House Near the Dead End
Eliseo (San Antonio, Texas)

I was born and raised in the small town of Mathis, Texas. It's located in south Texas some 50 miles from the coast. I spent my formative years in a small yellow house at a dead end. Our little dead end street was surrounded by thick brush, cacti and gnarled mesquite trees. It was here that I experienced many strange sightings, and heard sounds that I found hard to explain. Sounds in the kitchen became a nightly occurrence. It sounded as if somebody was shifting the dishes back and forth needlessly in the dish wrack. These noises happened so often they simply became a background noise that went largely unnoticed. At a young age many of the occurrences seemed to be quite normal and warranted no questions; while other experiences at the house, would later terrified me.

I had a tendency to go outside with my siblings to stargaze and walk about at night. On one such night, I was outside alone and this nightly need to explore the large world, turned to terror as I neared the mesquite woods. I was walking along the dark wooded area, when I suddenly felt the all too eerie feeling of being watched. I stood looking for a source: peering into the woods, I noticed a pair of glowing red eyes. They were nestled in the shadows between two large mesquite branches. The eyes seemed to hover at a very high altitude as if the "thing" hung in the trees looking down at me. Needless to say I was terrified, and doubled back inside. I explained to my mother that there was a large scary animal in the woods.

One of the most common apparitions I witnessed were shadow figures. I saw the shadows of people walking by our windows very often. They never really bothered me, until one night. I was lying in bed with my mother who, unfortunately, had fallen fast asleep before me. The master bedroom looked directly into the living room where, located in the center, was a long glass coffee table. Turning about trying to find a comfortable position, I momentarily glanced into the living room. Something caught my eye. Curious, I turned my focus to the living room and saw a shadow of a man standing in the center of the room. The figure stood there for a few seconds, turned, and quickly walked away towards the hallway—paying no heed to the glass coffee table that should have impeded his movement. Terrified, I quickly threw the sheets over my head and tried my hardest to fall asleep.

My teen years brought a few other unexplained experiences that happened while I was wide awake. Though I had long since stopped seeing the shadow people, I began seeing a tall white male with short blonde hair who would periodically walk by our front window. The first couple of times I saw him, I thought maybe a stranger had wandered into our yard. I would open the front door to glance outside only to find nobody.

None of these experiences would prepare me for the most terrifying experience that was yet to come.

I was home alone reading in my room one night, and I heard a noise that at first sounded distant but very distinct. It was the sound of a wagon being pulled by a horse. At first I barely noticed it as my full attention was on the book. The noise grew louder. My focus on the book swayed as my interest in a passing wagon was sparked. I chalked it up to maybe some kind of oddly timed Amish excursion in the middle of the night. I didn't think too hard on the matter. The noise grew louder and louder as if the wagon was moving down our street to the dead end. Now I was confused: why would a wagon come down this way? It simply made no sense. I wasn't scared yet, just curious. I put down my book, walked over to the window and peaked through the blinds. To my surprise I saw nothing. I clearly heard a wagon being pulled by a horse. I was dumbfounded. I thought for a second maybe somebody left the TV on in the living room. My hopes for a simple answer were quickly crushed as the sound of the wagon grew closer. I stepped back and cowered in the corner waiting for a horse and wagon to burst through my window. The wagon was now just outside my window. I could hear the wheels slowly turning in the dirt and the sound of hooves as they hit the ground. The wagon was now in my house. For the first time and only time in my life I was petrified. The wagon crept through windows and into the living room. Making its way through the kitchen and out the back ignoring any boundaries set by our house's walls.

Able to move again, I made my way to the back of the house and looked out the window. I could still hear the wagon creeping away into the night.

I would later share my experience with my mother. She responded, unsurprised by my tale, claiming she and one of my aunts had heard the very same thing one night while next door. This revelation blew my mind. For a few months I thought maybe I was going crazy, but now I have confirmation that I was not the only person who experienced the strange happening.

Upon further investigation, I found that long before the town had been established there was a network of cattle trails—and even a fort—not far north. It was built on the banks of the Nueces River by the army to protect settlers from Comanche raids. Maybe the wagon was simply an echo from the not too distant past. Whatever the wagon was, it was certainly very real to me that night.

I have since moved away from my old home. The old mesquite woods have been cut down. Houses are now on every side. I have never again experienced any of the strange happenings that plagued the little yellow house near the dead end.

Anything Ghost Show, Episode #241

The Drowning Premonition, and the Girl Entity
Kate (California, U.S.)

I live in a community in southern California and my house sits on the bay. Every year there is a Christmas boat parade with about thirty boats and yachts that are decked out in Christmas decorations—super whimsical and fun.

The night of the boat parade I had a nightmare. In this dream, I saw a face of an older female floating in water—no expression on her face, and the only color I could see was a blue hue. I instantly felt terror and somehow convinced myself to wakeup.

The next night I was browsing news articles on Facebook when I came across an article that made my heart want to jump out of my chest. The article was about a party-goer who attended a boat parade party on a yacht—in my neighborhood!—that was found dead in the bay. I then did some digging on Google, and I found that a 59-year-old woman had fallen off a yacht and drowned. This lady drowned a mile away from my house! I still don't understand why I saw her in my dreams that night.

My second story took place over ten years ago. I woke up one night and felt like someone was staring at me. As I sat up in bed, my eyes took a moment to adjust, and for a split second I thought I was still half asleep. I rubbed my eyes and then I saw her. She looked to be anywhere between five to seven years old; she was wearing a white dirty nightgown (it had dirt all over it). This little girl looked like a younger version of the girl from the ring that crawled out of the well.

The moment the entity noticed I saw her she cocked her head to the side— that to me was the creepiest of all things. Instead of getting out of bed and running out of my room I threw the blanket over my head. I sat there for what felt like forever. When I finally had the courage, I threw the blankets off and ran to the light switch. I had a hard time falling back to sleep that night.

Unfortunately, I wasn't the only one who saw this entity. My younger sister saw her one evening walking down the hallway, and then crawl under her bed. She was really traumatized by that incident, and it resulted in her sleeping in my room for months.

Lastly our grandmother saw this girl as well; but surprisingly, she wasn't scared when she saw the entity.

We eventually moved from that condo, a place that my family and I had other paranormal incidents happen to us.

Anything Ghost Show, Episode #245

The Limping Woman of Dripping Springs
Sam (Austin, Texas)

About fifteen years ago, I lived in Dripping Springs, near Austin, in the Texas Hill Country. The area is rolling hills, covered by live oak and juniper forests. My wife had horses on our property as a hobby, but keeping them was expensive, so she started a side business selling saddles and other horse equipment.

One autumn night, my wife asked me to deliver some horse tackle to a customer who lived out in the country. I had a cell phone, but this was before smart phones with maps, so I went out without a clear idea of how to get there, and I ended up getting lost. I remember going down a road that crossed a stream. In the moonlight, I could see the water going over the road, but I nervously crossed it and eventually arrived at a ranch with towers flanking the entrance.

The towers had live flames at the top—which was creepy but interesting to me. Realizing I was lost, I tried to get back to where the stream crossed the road. My attempts to get back kept retuning me to the gate with the flaming towers. After three attempts, I finally got to the stream crossing, and managed to get a cell phone signal to call my wife and ask for better directions.

A few weeks later she asked me to deliver a saddle at night and I refused at first—not wanting to get lost again. She told me that the address was in the town of Wimberley (not in the country), so it would be easier to find. Also, this was an expensive saddle, and the woman buying it had previously backed out of the purchase, so she wanted to make the sale before this woman changed her mind again.

I reluctantly agreed. But sure enough, I had trouble finding the place, and by the time I had delivered the saddle it was past 10 PM; so I had to drive back home down a very dark and desolate country road—and this time there was no moonlight.

Driving in the dark, I was nervous about hitting a deer (which had happened to me earlier that year), so I drove slowly—with my attention on the woods to each side. It was then that I noticed a woman walking with a limp on the side of the road, moving in the same direction I was. She was wearing a dress and walked gingerly—as though she was in pain. I slowed down and pulled up just ahead of her. Something felt very wrong and I immediately suspected this might be a carjacking attempt, and that the woman might be a decoy (with bad guys hiding in the woods). So, I kept my car locked, and only rolled down the window far enough to talk to the woman.

I asked her if she was okay, and she said she had been injured in a car crash and needed a ride into town. My first thought was, "What car crash?" (as I had not noticed any cars on the side of the road—and, because of my fear for hitting a deer, I had been very watchful).

I told her as much, and asked her where the car was. She said it was on another road. I then asked her if anyone else was involved in the crash and needed help. She said her son and daughter-in-law had been in the car that crashed but were not hurt and were already gone. She then said that they had crashed the car on purpose to try to kill her, but that she had survived. She then asked me to let her in and give her a ride into town.

Again, something felt very wrong, so I told her I couldn't but that I would call 911 for her. She immediately said, "No! Don't call anyone! Just give me a ride!"

I pulled away and stopped down the road long enough to call 911. As I traveled home, I passed an ambulance heading in the direction from where I had come. Something tells me they did not find her.

A couple of years ago, I told this story at an office Halloween party. A colleague who now lives in that area said, "Oh, that was the crazy lady of Dripping Springs. She is known for hitchhiking and attacking the people who give her rides. She has been in and out of mental institutions and jails."

Well, probably so. The woman did sound very real and not like a ghost. But what would even a crazy person be doing in the middle of nowhere late at night?

Anything Ghost Show, Episode #241

The Biker
Jon (U.S.)

This happened to my girlfriend and her family in the Ozark foothills of Missouri. I was at work one afternoon when she called me. She was sobbing, clearly upset. When I asked her what was wrong, she sobbed and told me she had just seen a dead body. Little by little, over the course of an hour or so, she got out the sequence of events the best she could.

She had gone to visit her father and brother who lived the next town over in the rural boot-heel of Missouri. She went over early in the morning to have breakfast with them. The plan was to meet up at her father's house in the countryside and he would drive them all into town to their favorite diner downtown.

They all piled into his Mustang and set out along the curvy back road that looped through the foothills into town. It wasn't long past dawn, and the sun was barely above the tree line. There was no traffic. They didn't pass a single other vehicle.

About five minutes from the city limit, they spotted someone standing on the shoulder of the road. As they neared this person, it became clear that it was a man with his back to them. He was wearing a leather jacket and dark pants; and as they approached they could tell he was dressed as a biker.

Something definitely wasn't right with this man. My girlfriend's dad slowed down so they could get a better look. As they got nearer, he didn't turn around and kept his back to their approaching car—and held his body in a strange posture. It gave my girlfriend the chills, because his stance wasn't at all normal. All he did the entire time they approached was point down, away from the road, toward the low side of the embankment where the road dropped off sharply.

Thinking the man was in some kind of trouble, my girlfriend's dad decided to see if he could help. He slowed down as they passed the man, and pulled off the road just ahead of him.

When they got out of the car and turned around to where the man had been...they faced an empty road.

The man had vanished.

They walked over to where he had been standing and looked down the steep embankment to where he had been pointing. In the ditch below they saw the body of man, lying twisted next to the wreckage of a motorcycle. His body was swollen and had obviously been there for several hours. He was wearing the same clothes as the man who had been standing on the shoulder of the highway.

When the highway patrol arrived they determined the biker had wiped out in a sharp curve in middle of the night, when no other vehicles were around. My girlfriend's family told the trooper about seeing the other man standing on the side of the hill. None of them knew what to make of it.

Between my girlfriend and I, we ended up at the uneasy conclusion that the ghost of the dead biker hadn't understood what had happened to him, and had stood by the roadside trying to get help. When someone finally stopped, he just didn't know what to do, and went to wherever we all go next.

I still don't know what any of this means, but it will haunt me as long as I live, and I hope something like that never happens to me.

Anything Ghost Show, Episode #245

The Hat Man in Minneapolis
John (Chicago, Illinois)

Although I live in Chicago now, I grew up in Minnesota. During the summer between my freshman and sophomore years of college, my then-girlfriend and I went for a late-night walk near her house in Minneapolis. We were walking around her block that was next to a hilly street by Lake Calhoun. Since it was past midnight, there was no one else around. As we were nearing the corner that we'd take to get back to her house, I noticed a figure in the distance coming down the hill.

The street was lit with lamps, but the figure (which appeared to be a man), was far enough away that we couldn't make out any features. We could only see that he was wearing a top hat, a coat with a cape, and was walking with a cane. I found it odd, but perhaps not that unusual that some eccentric type, or maybe an actor returning from a performance, would be walking home at that time.

I knew my girlfriend would probably find it upsetting if I brought attention to him, so I tried to act like I didn't find it odd. But I could tell she thought it was strange, and we started walking a little more quickly. As he walked down the hill and got closer to us, I realized I still couldn't make out any of his features: he was solid black, almost like a walking shadow.

"I'm freaked out," my girlfriend said, confirming that she was observing the same thing I was.

"It's probably okay," I said, trying to be reassuring.

This next part is the most difficult to explain: the man began getting closer to us at unnatural intervals of movement—he was seemingly skipping several feet at a time as he moved more quickly in our direction.

"Let's run!" she said. So we took off around the corner and ran into her house without looking back.

I knew what we had seen was unusual, but at the time, I was still thinking maybe it was just some weirdo out for a late-night prank. The fact that we both saw him move in the same way, though, gave me pause. She was crying and really shaken by the incident. The daughter of an Episcopal priest, she insisted that we pray to prevent the figure from reaching us. Finding it a little silly, I nonetheless said a prayer to keep us from any harm.

I had practically forgotten about this whole episode when, a few years later, I remembered it and thought I'd Google the figure—to see if anything showed up. I was shocked to find information not just about Shadow People, which fit what we saw uncannily, but about the Hat Man. So many others have reported seeing exactly what we had: a shadow person wearing a hat and coat, solid black with no features, coming toward them.

The details of our encounter, though, seemed a little different from most: we saw him as college students, not children; he was wearing Victorian clothes, not a fedora, as seems to be most common; we were together when we saw him, not alone; and we were outside, not in a bedroom, where he seems to show most often. There was no possibility that we dreamed it, since we were wide-awake and walking outside. But the general descriptions matched so closely with what I saw that I certainly believe the Hat Man was who we encountered.

As best as I can tell, its appearance to people seems to correlate with something traumatic or terrible happening in the person's life. I can't think of anything in particular in our lives that it might have been signifying—except for the fact that each of our sets of parents ended up getting divorced within the next couple of years? Perhaps that was a powerful enough soon-to-be tragic occurrence we had in common that the Hat Man appeared to both of us?

I'm happy to say that I've never seen him again, but I remain fascinated by this figure, and the fact that so many seem to have seen it. I'd be curious to hear if any additional Anything Ghost listeners have had similar encounters.

Anything Ghost Show, Episode #229

Child Ghost in Photo

Philip (Tucson, Arizona)

During the first week of February, my folks adopted a dog from the local pound. Once they brought the dog home, they wanted to send a picture of it to my siblings and myself (my parents are retirees and my siblings and I all live in different places). So my folks went outside to their backyard to take a couple of pictures.

My mom sat in a patio chair and held the dog in her lap, and my dad attempted to take the picture. Unfortunately, my dad is a total Luddite and somehow put the phone in selfie mode and shot a quick video of himself trying to fiddle with the camera. My dad finally figured the phone out and took a few pics, and then they went inside.

While they were reviewing the pictures, they noticed something perplexing: while watching the playback of the video, they noticed a person walking directly behind my dad!

Here's the thing, there's no ethereal quality to the person. Besides a bizarre gait, it's just an obvious person. You can hear footsteps before it even comes into view, too. It's so clear that it all looks matter of fact. But there was NO WAY, anyone was there other than my parents. Again, my folks are retirees and live alone. The video was shot in my parents' private backyard—which is surrounded by a brick wall. So it's not like a pedestrian just happened to be walking by while he was fumbling around with the camera.

Even if it was a person, my mom (as well as the dog) would have seen it— they were sitting in a chair facing my dad, and they didn't see a thing.

My dad almost deleted the video without watching it, but luckily he decided to give it a once over.

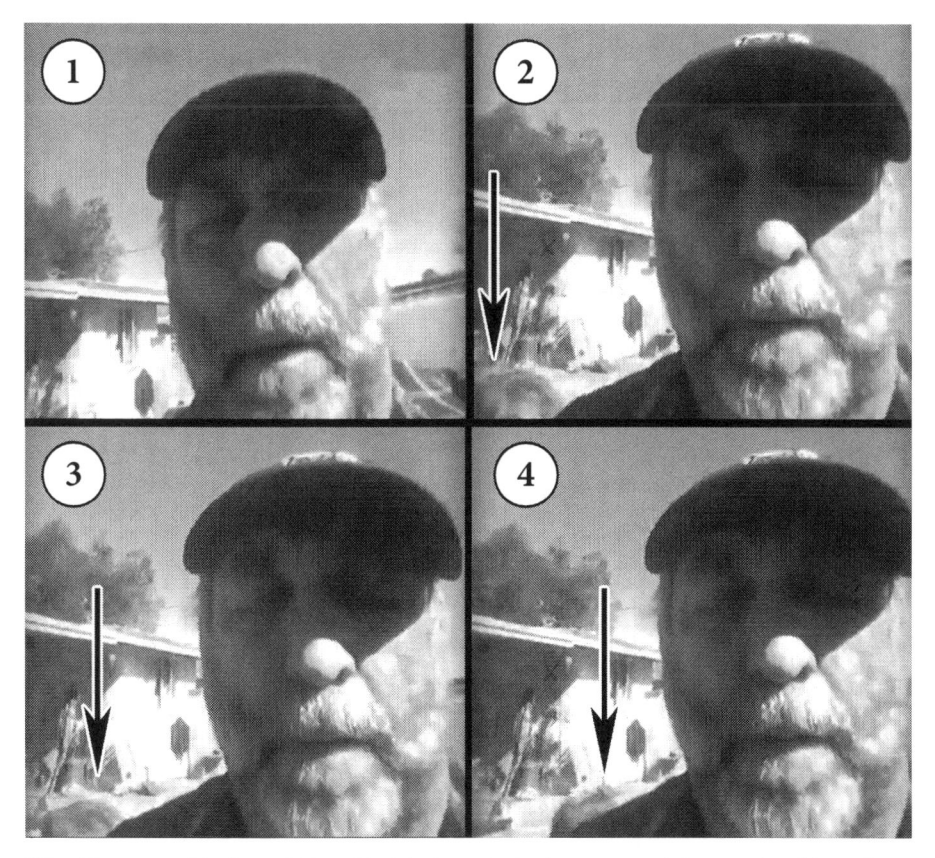

His wife was seated in front of him with their dog; nobody else was around; it was a fenced-in yard. Video is available on YouTube (as of book release date): https://youtu.be/WdpM5j9cRSk

Anything Ghost Show, Episode #245

The Digging Witch in Yuma, Arizona
Martha (Arizona, U.S.)

I had been living with my mom at my nana & tata's house for two years at the time this experience happened.

I was standing close to an open curtained window in my grandfather's room with my mom (who was using the natural light to do a decent job of brushing and styling my hair for a school day in my Kindergarten year). It was probably a very routine morning, that is, until I saw a face in the window.

It was not an ordinary face, it was a face that I could only equate to that of a witch's face. She had greenish gray skin, long scraggly hair and freaky eyes that seemed to glow and twirl in the oddest manner. I don't know if at first I screamed, and then was quietly transfixed, or the opposite; but when I wouldn't respond to my Mom's questioning (she didn't see anything but did say I pointed at the window), my mom ran outside to investigate, but saw nothing out of the ordinary.

As she was outside looking into what could be causing me so much anxiety, this witch lady was hovering back and forward to the window, knowing fully well she was scaring the daylights out of me. When she hovered farther away from the window, she'd immediately began digging a hole in the ground and pointing at it—giving me the most grimacing smile you can imagine. I have no idea how long this encounter lasted, but she did eventually fade away, and my mom came back to tell me she saw nobody outside at all.

I have no idea why our family dog, who was out in the yard, didn't bark not even once? I told Mom that I saw a witch, and that she was digging a hole and pointing and laughing at me. She said she saw no witch and no hole whatsoever.

After that incident, I made sure not to have those curtains open all the way. This was the first of many spooky things I've experienced at my grandparent's house in Yuma, Arizona.

Anything Ghost Show, Episode #241

Chapter Eight

Schools

And as the moon from some dark gate of cloud
Throws o'er the sea a floating bridge of light,
Across whose trembling planks our fancies crowd
Into the realm of mystery and night,—

(Poem Continues in Chapter 9)

"Don't Touch My Home!"
Sarah (Canada)

This happened around ten years ago when I was working at a small Montessori school.

One day at lunchtime, a police car, fire truck and ambulance came blaring up the street and went to the house across the street. At first it didn't seem too unusual (an elderly woman had died alone in her house), but later we learned of the circumstances.

The lady had been a recluse. She was paranoid schizophrenic and had died months prior—she froze to death on the kitchen floor when the boiler broke. She had cut herself off from her friends and family; and the neighbours had called the police when they noticed the mail stacking up, as well as a foul smell coming from the house.

She hadn't changed her will, so her ex-husband, who lived in Ottawa, inherited the house; but the home was in such bad condition that he had to call in a clean up crew that specialized in cleaning up crime scenes.

Since the school I worked at was across the street from the lady's house, we got to know the crew. They were friendly, and were always waving to the children.

One day, they showed up but were unable to unlock the front door. They were using the same keys that they'd had been using for the last two weeks, but nothing worked. These guys were big burley guys who just wanted to get the job done. They came over to the school and asked if they could use the phone (this was slightly before cell phones were common), and they called to ask what to do. The ex-husband told them that one the neighbours had an extra set of keys.

They got the second set of keys (that had a key to the back door as well), but sure enough, the key went in the lock, but it did not unlock the door—on both the front door and back door. They finally decided to slide a window open and go in that way; and the next day, the keys worked perfectly.

For the next few weeks, the workers told us other stories of strange things that went on in the house from workers feeling like they were being shoved to lights going on and off.

My coworker lived close by and could see the house from her bedroom and she said she would frequently see all the lights off at night and then at midnight or later, the bedroom light of the house would be on.

When the cleaning was finished, the house went on the market and sold for almost one million dollars. A family with children moved in and ended up enrolling their children in the school. Some of the teachers couldn't wait to ask them if they'd been having any paranormal experiences, and wanted to tell them the whole history of the house. They were well aware of what had happened previously, but said that it was just a regular house, no hauntings.

My personal feeling is that somehow this woman's spirit was trying to keep the workers out of her house. Since she was a hoarder, the workers just threw out all of the junk; if you have ever watched any of the hoarder shows, people get very attached to their hoard, so I believe, from beyond the grave, she was telling them to keep out of her house.

Anything Ghost Show, Episode #229

The White Figures That I See
Claude (Stellenbosch, South Africa)

It all started when I was around nine years old. I was sitting in class at the end of the day listening to the story my teacher was reading. While staring out the window like I always did (because my class looked out over the rugby field), I noticed a white figure floating towards the class from a house that was next to the school. The figure came and sat down in the windowsill, and stayed there until my teacher stopped reading; when she was done, it went back to wherever it came from.

For the rest of the year, every time it was story time the figure would come floating towards the class and it seemed to be listening to the story. At the time I didn't really believe in ghosts and the like, so I wrote it off as a trick of the light.

But then I started to see similar things in other parts of town and at various times of day and night. I eventually started looking for them and I noticed that they hang around particular people or places. They have no distinguishable features, although it does seem that they are human-like beings wearing white cloaks.

I told my mother about it when my grandmother died, because at her funeral there were many of these beings hanging around the grave with their heads bowed as if paying their respects. My mother then told me that my grandmother always used to speak about the exact same things before her mind started to slip when she had her second stroke when I was very young.

I have to say that up until September last year I have never been frightened by these figures, I always feel very peaceful when they're around. But around my nineteenth birthday last year I was woken up by what sounded like my radio. When I checked it, the radio was off and I got back in bed thinking I must have been dreaming. The moment I put my head back down on the pillow the "radio voice" started again right next to my head. I wasn't so much scared as I was startled, but I quickly calmed down again when I turned to see one of these figures sitting on it's knees next to my bed facing away from me. I couldn't understand what it was saying, but I got the idea that it maybe didn't know I was there and was off on it's own mission. It stayed there for a while speaking to itself, then disappeared into thin air.

I have not gone up to one and spoken to it or tried to see if it acknowledges me, despite seeing one at least once a day for the last couple of years. Do you have any idea what these figures might be and what they are doing when they hang around specific people or places?

Anything Ghost Show, Episode #227

Haunted Rehearsals
Jake (Aberdeen, Scotland)

I was part of my university's charity committee, and each year we would write and produce a musical to be put on at the city's biggest theatre. It's been a tradition for almost a hundred years, and raises tens of thousands of pounds each time.

Our rehearsals would always take place at Marischal (pronounced "marshal") College. Marischal is the second biggest granite structure in the world, and sits right in the middle of the city. With the exception of a small museum and a hall used for graduations, much of the building was empty and in a state of disrepair. Don't get me wrong, it's stunningly beautiful, but with a history going back to the 1800s, there was a certain foreboding atmosphere in certain areas—and as we were getting our show ready, we were living in this atmosphere 10 AM to 10 PM every day for a 4 week period.

Marischal has its fair share of ghost stories going back decades and we'd tell the same ones every year. There was the organ in the graduation hall that some swore would play by itself; there was the staircase leading down to the old mortuary with all manner of alleged night-time odours; and my personal favourite: for reasons we'll come to, had always been the lecturer who died from a heart attack after being blindfolded and subjected to a mock trial by students in the old debating chamber. They say that he was sentenced to death and that the students would complete the prank by whipping him with a wet towel. But when he fell after the first blow, the joke was over. Now, tell a group of 30 students that there's a ghost with a grudge in this largely abandoned building and you can imagine the nervousness from some when they were alone. Thankfully, I never fully bought into these stories at first—otherwise, I wager I'd have reacted quite differently when I had my own experience.

That, however, wasn't the end of it.

Once I got back upstairs, it was time to change into my costume. Being generally shy and not wanting anyone to walk in on me half-naked, I took my things to the very top of the same staircase. This was to a gallery overlooking the graduation hall, and not somewhere anyone usually went. I stayed in the stairwell and started to change. After a minute, I heard footsteps coming up the stairs below me. It sounded like someone slowly coming up from the very bottom floor. I didn't think much of it at first, but as the steps got closer, I looked out over the banister and said, "Someone changing up here!"

I didn't see anyone, but this wasn't unusual, as the space between the banisters heading down didn't afford much of a view of the stairs. I started to put my top on and, while my vision was blocked, I heard the person pass the main floor and start to climb to where I was.

"Still getting changed, I wouldn't come up," I said.

But as I pulled the t-shirt down, no one was there and I could still hear the footsteps. They walked right past me; going over the spot I stood on and headed out onto the gallery.

I grabbed the rest of my things, ran down the stairs as fast as I could, and out into our rehearsal area—almost knocking over our director as she came through. She could see something was up, and when I asked if anyone else was around, she assured me that we were quite alone. I never told her the full story.

A short epilogue to this story:

A few weeks later, I mentioned what happened to my mother. She had been part of the same group twenty-five years earlier, and I knew she loved the building. As I told her the story, she started to smile. She told me that, as an infant, she'd occasionally take me to rehearsals with her. One time, she let a couple of the students take care of me and they brought me into the debating chamber. I was left there for a few minutes, and when they came back, I was sitting all alone, giggling and interacting with someone they could not see. They chalked it up to me having an imaginary friend. But now, I'm not so sure.

Anything Ghost Show, Episode #226

The Ghost on the Stage

Alyssa (Wyoming, Michigan)

This story takes place in my high school in mid December of last year. My boyfriend invited me to watch him rehearse for a play that he was going to be in. I agreed to watch him rehearse with everyone else, as long as my best friend was going to be there. So I watched him rehearse the Little Mermaid with everyone else.

Soon after he was done, he went to get a drink from the vending machine—this was after everyone had left, including the director of the play (who had left to use the bathroom before locking up).

I was left alone on the stage, so I decided to walk around a bit. I had just walked behind a curtain when I heard the door leading to the stage close. Thinking that it was my boyfriend (since he was closer to the stage than the play director), I called out for him, "Hey. I'm behind one of the curtains. Come find me!" I've always messed around like that with him.

But when I didn't get a reply, I started to become nervous. So I stepped outside of the curtain I was hiding behind, and peered towards the door that led to the stage. There I saw a little girl (who looked to be maybe eight years old), holding a stuffed teddy bear and crying. I felt sad and curious because as far as I knew no one was supposed to be in the school besides my boyfriend, the play director and myself.

I don't know what made me do it but, I walked up to the little girl. When I went to wipe a tear that was falling down from her cheek my hand went right through her. She then disappeared and my boyfriend walked in through stage door. I was in complete shock and when he asked me what was wrong. I told him that I had just stubbed my toe.

I have never shared this story with anyone, and I'm hoping that when I go to rehearse for the new school play next year, I won't have to deal with another situation like that.

Anything Ghost Show, Episode #224

The Maid at Christchurch Mansion in Suffolk, U.K.

Danny (U.K.)

When I was seven years old, I attended a school trip to a historic mansion in Suffolk, UK. This mansion is known for its ghostly apparitions and strange occurrences. I didn't know about the history of ghosts at that time, as I was so young, and it wasn't until my later years that I learned of other sightings that have been reported there.

It was a bright and sunny day when we arrived at the mansion, and all of us were in high spirits—excited to explore this grand building. Once inside, I remember being amazed at all of the wall hangings, the furniture and—being a young boy at the time—I was particularly taken by the suits of armour and weaponry.

While we were wandering the halls, I lost sight of my teacher and started searching frantically. When I went to look behind me, I saw a lady with her back to me. I thought it was my teacher, so I breathed a sigh of relief, and instantly felt safe again.

The lady was walking down the corridor, so I followed (as I didn't want to get lost again). Then she turned right, into one of the rooms. I noticed there was a rope barrier across the door that said, "Do Not Enter." I didn't pay the sign any attention, as I figured if that was the way my teacher went, then we must be permitted through there. I followed her into the room and past the rope barrier. But as I was about three or four steps into the room, I heard my teacher call out to me from the doorway I had just walked through. I whipped around and saw my teacher standing behind me. I turned back to the lady I had just followed, and she was gone—despite there being no other exits.

My teacher was trying to usher me out of the room, telling me that we were not allowed in there: saying it was time to go, and I had to get back to my classmates.

I spent the next twenty years trying to piece everything together. That's when I recalled her outfit: she was wearing a black dress with a white apron tied around the waist; and a white bonnet on her head with her hair pulled back.

I've been back to the mansion on countless occasions: speaking to staff and inquiring about the lady; and it was confirmed that others have seen the same maid wandering the halls.

I sometimes wonder if the maid appeared to me because she knew I felt lost. Perhaps she was guiding me back to my teacher.

Anything Ghost Show, Episode #248

Chapter Nine

Workplace

So from the world of spirits there descends
A bridge of light, connecting it with this,
O'er whose unsteady floor, that sways and bends,
Wander our thoughts above the dark abyss.

Haunted Houses (1858)
by Henry Wadsworth Longfellow, 1807-1882

Ghost Patrol
Sgt. Mike (Ohio, U.S.)

I've been a police officer for approximately seventeen years. When I first graduated from the police academy, I got a job with a small suburb just outside of Cleveland, Ohio. Because there was very little crime inside the city, and I was a young officer, I spent most of my time running traffic on the highway (working the midnight shift).

One cold January night about 2:30 AM, I was traveling eastbound heading to my favorite spot to run radar. While en route, I saw a female walking westbound. Seeing people walking down the side of the highway is not unusual: sometimes their cars would run out of gas, or break down. I only saw the female for a brief time as I was traveling about 70 MPH in the opposite direction (and a grass medium separated east and west bound lanes). I called the female into our dispatch center and gave the mile marker where I saw the female walking.

I traveled up the highway for about two minutes, and turned around to make contact with the female. I found it odd that I did not see her vehicle on the side of the highway broken down, while I traveled to the turn-a-around. I remember thinking she must have been cold walking that far.

Anyway, I turned around and spotlighted the area, but failed to locate the female. I had no idea where she could have gone. I know it was a physical impossibility that she made it to the next exit ramp—because it was four miles away. On the side of the highway was a fenced-in wooded area. From the time I saw her, turned around and made it to her location, less than five minutes had passed.

I shrugged it off and went on my way, until I met up with some veteran officers for lunch about 5:00 AM. They asked me about what I saw. I explained that I didn't get a good look at her face, but noticed that she had long blonde hair and was skinny. They informed me that several years ago (long before cell phones), a female had run out of gas and was walking along the side off the highway. She was struck and killed by a passing car in the same area. The officers further stated that they get calls regarding a female walking in that area of the highway at night; they give the same description, but we are never able to locate her.

I thought the veteran cops were trying to scare me because I was new to the force, but that changed when I walked into the dispatch center and talked with one of our oldest dispatchers. She confirmed they actually do receive calls about a female walking in that area, at that time of night. She pulled up records of callers calling in about her, and giving the same description that I gave.

I never saw her again for the two years while I worked at that department. I'm still a police officer in a much larger city but I still think about that night sometimes. *Anything Ghost Show, Episode #250*

The Haunted Old Mill Bakery
Michelle (New York, U.S.)

Many years ago, when I was in college, I worked part time at a small family owned bakery in Upstate NY. I've always been an artistic type and I was excited to be training with the owner's daughter to become a cake decorator.

The bakery was located next to a large creek, and the back of the building was an old stone mill that had been renovated—it housed the ovens, bread mixers, freezers, and bread racks. The front of the bakery and storefront was a simple brick building that had been an add-on some years later.

During the busy graduation and wedding seasons, I was often asked to go in on Sunday to catch up on cake orders. The family regularly attended church on Sunday, and the bakery was not open. I liked working alone and needed the pay, so I didn't mind doing this from time to time.

It was during these times that I first discovered there was a heaviness in the air at the bakery. Usually the place was humming with workers, music was playing on the radio, and customers were chatting away out in the dining area. On Sundays it was quiet and still.

There were two swinging pantry doors that separated the old mill portion of the bakery from the area where we decorated cakes and the storefront. I soon found myself avoiding going beyond those swinging doors at all costs. Once beyond the doors, there was a noticeable change in the air. It was thick and heavy, and felt as if it were pressing on me. Immediately I would feel as if a thousand eyes were staring at me—even though I knew the building was empty.

One Sunday afternoon I was decorating a cake, and I distinctly heard the side door (which was around the corner and down a small hallway), open and slam shut. I felt a breeze of warm air rush into the bakery from the outside. I glanced up from the cake I was working on (expecting to see the owner's daughter who told me she may be stopping by), yet, there was no one there. The side door was a huge metal door, it had a distinct sound when opened and did not open easily. I stopped what I was doing and looked around the bakery for who had opened the door—I even peeked out into the parking lot. There was nobody there except me. Though shaken, I mustered enough courage to finish the cake and went home immediately afterwards.

Some time passed before the next incident; since then I had convinced myself it was lack of sleep that caused me to think the door had opened and shut own its own. It was another quiet Sunday afternoon, and I was working alone again. I had a whole table full of graduation cakes that I was decorating. As I was piping butter cream roses on the corners of a sheet cake, I heard a man's voice, as clear as a bell, come from the dining area, "Hello??? Excuse me?"

Every hair on the back of my neck stood up. I dropped my piping bag and peered out into the dining area: No one was there. I was quite shaken, and unable to finish my work. I put everything away the best I could and left immediately.

A few days later, during the week, I was decorating cakes along side the owner's daughter. I decided to tell her what had happened on Sunday, because it was bothering me so much. I didn't know what she would think—perhaps that I was crazy. Instead, she very casually shrugged, and said, "Well, that doesn't sound too bad. Have you seen the shadow people yet?"

She proceeded to tell me about shadow figures that resided in the old mill portion of the bakery. Both she and her family had seen child sized black shadows darting between the bread racks. Her mother was passing by at that moment and agreed the bakery was a very haunted place, and didn't realize that I didn't already know about it.

It is true the stone mill portion of the bakery was very old, and I am sure there is some history there. Though, I've been unable to find any information on it. I do know the area was formally a river settlement inhabited by the Mohawk and Oneida (Native American) tribes before British colonists began to inhabit the area.

At any rate, the family seemed to be at peace with it, and it continues to be a productive family owned business to this day.

Anything Ghost Show, Episode #236

Haunted Retirement Home
Heather (Washington, U.S.)

I've worked at a retirement home for about eight months. It's a very rewarding job and I have great relationships with my residents. It's hard to tell sometimes if things that happen here are genuine experiences, or signs of the mental decline of people who live here. I've asked lots of my coworkers about things that have happened, and only a few of them have told me some things. Recently, a few creepy things have happened to me and that is why I decided to write to you.

The first thing that I was told was a story about a resident who would sit in our dining room (it fits about 120 people) and shout about the lady who was watching her. This lady apparently sat in the corner by an art piece and stared at her throughout dinner. No one else saw her—and the resident's declining mental state is very likely to blame—but my coworker who told the story, said that the whole dining room was creeped out. Sometimes the resident wouldn't say anything, but she would stare at the spot where the lady would always be.

One night, during a fancier event when we were serving dinner, a coworker and I went down to the wine room to collect wine. His name was Mark and he had worked there for several years. We were chit chatting, I had been in the down stairs area a few times and it had creeped me out a lot. Somehow the conversation turned to weird things, and he told me that sometimes people claimed they'd seen a man down there. Before I could think, I blurted out "a man without a face, right?"

He looked shaken. I don't know why I said it. I hadn't seen the man, but every time I'd been down there, I had a feeling of a man without a face being down there.

"How did you know that?" He asked.

"I don't know, I just felt like that's who was down here."

"Did Kenneth put you up to this?" He asked seriously. Kenneth was a co-worker. Mark thought I was pulling his leg or something.

"No I had no idea that's what people saw I just...felt like there was a faceless man down here."

We were both creeped out: me having my feelings confirmed, and him believing I was joking around with him.

I still haven't seen the faceless man, but I get a feeling of him whenever I go into that storage area.

The last thing that happened is the reason that I'm writing you. Sometimes during the week I work an early morning shift where I am basically alone in the dining room for several hours. I keep myself busy and listen to podcasts with headphones. It's very relaxing. Recently, I've been hearing whispering during these shifts. Sometimes I'll take some breaks and stop listening to my headphones and I'll hear whispering. I've tried so hard to debunk these whispers; I thought maybe it was coming through my headphones but it isn't. I thought maybe other people had left their phone on, but no. I've checked the fire stairs to see if people are talking in them, but it isn't that either. It always seems to be when I'm alone. No one else has heard them. I can't hear what they're saying but I'm hoping it stays that way.

Anything Ghost Show, Episode #225

Ghost Boy at the Zoo
William (New York, U.S.)

I work at a local zoo, and some of us who have worked there for awhile know that it is haunted; but, being a public family place, the zoo has chosen not to advertise the fact that it is indeed haunted—and not just by people...I've seen and experienced all sorts of strange things while there. This story is about a small ghost boy.

I've worked at the zoo for quite awhile; and throughout my years, I've caught glimpses of a ghost boy. He's around six or seven, dirty blonde hair, and is usually wearing the colors red and blue.

I remember the first time I saw him. I was operating a train ride, and there was only a woman and her daughter sitting about the middle of the train. I glanced back to be certain that they were seated before we started moving, I also noticed a boy sitting by himself in the last row. I knew I had only let the woman and her daughter on, so I glanced back again and the boy was gone and only the two remained.

I saw him on and off from that first time. It was usually on or around the train; since that was the area I worked the most, but occasionally I'd see him in other parts of the zoo.

One day a new employee asked me if the zoo was haunted. I asked her why she would ask a random question like that; she told me she saw a boy who fit the ghost's description to a tee, and he was there one moment and gone the next—with no explanation. I decided then that I could tell her the stories about what I had seen of him.

A few weeks later, she came up to me excitedly and said, "I know who he is!"

I was confused at first, because I had no clue who or what she was talking about, but then she said, "You know!" and it hit me.

"I looked up a name from one of the donation plaques, and it's got to be him! The pictures I found look just like him!" She exclaimed. "And, he died a few years before you started working here!"

When I got home that night, I looked up the name she had told me and sure enough he looks like an exact match.

From then on, instead of just thinking of him as "the ghost boy", when I see him I smile and whisper "Hi Simon."

Anything Ghost Show, Episode #233

Flying Basket

Lisa (U.K.)

I was working at a flat in a huge house in Harrogate North Yorkshire today. I've worked at the place weekly for a long time. While there, I'd never felt, or heard anything out of the ordinary. However, today I opened the door to the en-suite bathroom, and a basket flew across the room, hit the shower door, then fell to the floor. The room had no windows, and yet the basket flew across the room at eye level with me (I'm 5'2").

The weird thing was that I wasn't actually scared: I think I just couldn't process what I'd seen at first.

I texted the flat owner, "Something really weird has just happened here."

The owner rang me straight back, and I told him what had happened. I sent him a photo of where the basket had landed, and neither of us could explain it.

After a while I even tried asking "the ghost" out loud, to move the basket again if any body was there; I called out twice but the basket didn't move; then, I put the basket back to where it had been in the room, and opened the door really quickly to see if this would create a draught which would move the basket—it didn't move a millimetre!

I've thought of every scenario possible. But the fact is that the basket just flew from one side of the room to the other; and where it flew from was not where it was in the room in the first place.

I've always thought if I ever saw anything weird in a house that was working at, I'd be out of there like a shot—never to return. But I'm actually intrigued and keep wracking my brain for an explanation.

I'll be working there every Friday, so if anything else happens, I'll keep you posted.

"...a basket flew across the room, hit the shower door, then fell to the floor."

Anything Ghost Show, Episode #247

Confessions of a Fixer
Eric (Utah, U.S.)

This story is more about my friend Todd, than me. I've changed the names in the story, so those I know aren't affected by me sharing it.

I work inside a hospital in Utah for one of the largest healthcare companies in the west. Our office is located on the 2nd floor, directly above the emergency department. Our team is part of an emergency dispatch team: so if someone is having a medical emergency and needs to contact their doctor, they go through us. All our work is done over the phone and we're all stuck in one small room, so we get to know each other pretty well. Our job has two speeds: it's either utter chaos and complete confusion during our busy times, or it's completely dead during the slow times. During these down times we have to find ways to entertain ourselves.

My friend Todd was the one who introduced me to podcasts; I had no idea what they were—and specifically he introduced me to the Anything Ghost Show. Todd and I would listen to it together. Although, we couldn't listen to it out loud, so we had to listen to it, each through our own headphones (that's because company policy stated nothing was to be played out loud; but also because we had some skittish workers who wouldn't like to be hearing the show). So Todd and I would listen to the podcast together during the slow times. We'd often discuss the stories: which story made our B.S. meters go off, and which ones we really enjoyed. We'd pay special attention to anyone calling from Utah or Salt Lake—and tried to figure out where they were calling from, or what they were doing.

I'm not a disbeliever in the paranormal or ghosts, it's just something I've never given much thought to. I'm not a real logical guy either: I'm just not that into ghosts. But I listened to it because it was entertaining and enjoyable—I enjoyed the stories, even if I didn't particularly believe them. And it gave me something to do that kind of connected me to my co-worker: something we could talk about and do together—and it was an entertaining way to help pass those slow times at work.

One day about eighteen months ago (during one of our very busy times), my friend Todd pulled me aside and asked me if he could go home for the day (he said he wasn't feeling well). He had left early the day before, and he was kind of one of those guys who tended to leave work early more often than he should. As I said earlier, we were really busy at that time, so I said, "Dude, I don't think you can go now—is there anyway you can stay until the end of your shift?"

He wasn't very happy with that, but he agreed. He didn't talk to me the rest of the shift (obviously not happy that I had asked him to stay).

Our shift ended at 11 PM (that's when we had shift change), and we all headed home for the night.

I was at home later, about 3 or 3:30 AM, and was having a typical late dinner (unwinding from the day), when I got a call from the hospital. Now when someone calls from the hospital, it doesn't say who the call is from, it's just a general number from the hospital and doesn't say from where the call was routed. I assumed it was from my co-workers who had a question for me. This wasn't uncommon, as they knew they could call me with any questions or concerns—except between the hours of 7 AM and 2 PM: that's when I would get my sleep. So I picked up the phone, "Hello? Hello? Hello?!"

There was no response from the other side, just dead air, so I hung up and called the office. I got one of my co-workers and asked, "Hey. What's going on? Did you guys need something?"

The office told me they had not called, and that everything was fine.

I thought it was strange, but didn't think anything of it and went back to my dinner, and watched some TV.

It wasn't long before the phone began to ring again. But this time the phone call was coming from my friend Todd's phone. It wasn't the first time someone called me from their personal phone, but it was uncommon. So wondering what was going on, I picked up the phone, "Hello? Todd? Hello? Todd, are you there?"

Dead air, again.

I figured he most likely pocket dialed me. Not wanting to wake up his wife and kids in the middle of the night, I didn't call him back—if it was urgent, he would tell me about it later, or call me right back. So, I headed off to bed, and fell into a deep sleep.

I was started awake around 9 AM the next morning by my phone ringing. My family, friends and coworkers all know not to call me during my sleeping hours; the only person who would call me was my boss—and she would only call if it was something very important.

So half-asleep, I answered the early morning sleep-disturbing call: sure enough, it was my boss.

"Eric? Are sitting down?" She asked.

I groggily replied, "Ah, I'm laying down—I was sound asleep? What's going on?"

She told me that the night before, after my friend Todd got home from work, he complained to his wife about abdominal pains. The pains persisted and were so bad that he couldn't sleep (I thought to myself, "He really was sick"). His wife convinced him to go to the emergency room.

So it turned out, that about two hours after he left work, he was back at the very same hospital, in the room right below where had been working, and two hours after that…they pronounced him dead.

Todd had an aneurysm in the arteries of his spleen, and he had internal bleeding that the surgeons couldn't stop, so he died that very morning.

I was in shock—we all were. He was thirty-two and left behind a wife and two little kids. I just couldn't believe he was gone—it was such a blow to the whole team. It was then I knew, that I was not going to let ANYONE know that Todd had asked me if he could leave early the night before.

But I thought a lot about it—I thought a LOT about it.

What would have happened if I had let him go home earlier that night: "Yeah dude, take off."

If he had gone to the emergency room any sooner, could they have done anything—could anything have been changed?

Some things you can't think about too much, or it'll drive you crazy.

I'm kind of a fixer: when I see something is wrong, I like to fix it—and this couldn't be fixed. It was what it was; so I hid the story, and I didn't tell anybody what had happened—and I tried not to think too much about it.

So time went on, like it will, and we hired new employees (a replacement for Tom and some others). We all remembered him; grieved for him; but we talked about him less and less as time went by, and pretty soon we quit sharing our favorite Tom stories

Oh well, I've begun calling him by his real name and not by Todd—I apologize. His name isn't Todd, his name is Tom…his name was Tom.

Before I go on, I need to describe our workplace. As I mentioned earlier, we work on the second floor of a hospital, and it's the only non-patient floor in the hospital (so there are no patients where we work). It's a floor of offices where a bunch of people work, and there's also a cafeteria. So during the weekdays it's a very busy floor with all the workers going to and from the cafeteria. On the weekends, all the other offices are closed; the cafe is closed; and there is no house-keeping. So it's just our department tucked away in a little corner of the second floor (with seven-floors of patient care above us, and a bustling emergency room underneath us). The weekends on the second-floor were like a ghost town, and no one had any reason to come to the floor but us.

We were working on a Sunday afternoon about four months ago. The weekends are light, so there were only three of us working that day. Company policy states that at least two people must be available for phones at any time, so if someone had to leave, they had to go by themselves. Toward the latter part of the day, I wandered out of the office by myself to get myself something from the vending machine. I put some quarters in the vending machine, and pressed my selection. The machine decided to not give me my drink, so frustrated I begin lightly pounding on the machine—and tried to move it back and forth to get it to dispense the drink. As I was doing this, I heard a male voice coming from behind me say, "Well that sucks!"

At first I was embarrassed thinking, "Oh man, who's watching me in my futile attempt to shake this drink loose?"

I looked around me...there was nobody there. There was no way anyone could have snuck up on me because it was a silent, deserted, empty hall. But confused, I peered around the corner...nobody there. I also thought that maybe someone had passed me and had gone to the elevator: but I hadn't heard the doors open or the floor bell ding—or anything for that matter. It had been silent and empty. The only thing I heard was a voice that said, "Well that sucks."

As I said, I'm not a paranormal type guy, so the idea of a ghost didn't even enter my head. In fact, I just popped more money into the machine, got my drink and headed back to the office.

About forty-five minutes after getting back to work, my friend Josie went to the restroom. She was barely gone a minute, when she came rushing back into the office. She was pale and shaking like I've never seen—and slammed the door behind her.

"What's going on Josie? What's the problem?" I asked.

She told us that she was heading down the empty hall to the bathroom, and just as she was about to enter, she heard a male voice say, "I can SEE you!"

That totally freaked her out and she panicked; she hurried inside the bathroom and as she fumbled to get the door locked, she heard a giggling male voice coming from inside the bathroom say, "I'm in here, too."

She bolted herself from the bathroom that she was trying to barricade herself in, sprinted back to the office and slammed the door behind her.

After hearing her story, I realized how much it seemed to resemble what I had heard while at the vending machine. I told the two others about my experience, and we got ourselves all riled up—half excited, half giggling. This eventually lead to someone suggesting that one of us walk through the hall and record it with our phone camera—to see if we could catch anything on video.

Somehow (I don't recall how), I was recruited to do it. I probably volunteered as an excuse to get out of the room for a minute; plus, I wasn't buying the idea that there was something paranormal going on—and I thought it would be fun.

So I grabbed my phone and went out wandering down the halls, video taping and calling out, "Hello? Is there anybody there? Is anybody there?..." I video taped the halls, showing that everywhere was completely empty; I walked by the vending machine and then I headed around the corner to the bathroom. On the video, you can hear a little bit of noise before I opened the bathroom door, but I didn't notice that at the time.

I opened the door.

The atmosphere inside the restroom is very difficult to describe—mainly because I was only in there for a millisecond—I wasn't in there long at all. After I opened the door, I flipped on the light switch. Now, I've never been inside of a mobile home in a tornado, but that's how I would describe the sound inside the bathroom: there was a crazy, windy, swooshing tornado-like noise, and yet everything inside the bathroom was completely still—nothing was moving. But more than the sound, there was a feeling I got: anger, hatred, I was not wanted there—I wasn't supposed to be there. And I felt that the instant I stepped inside. I'm a big guy, and I'm not known for being a fast guy—or someone who can move swiftly. But I closed my phone, and made my way back down the hall pretty quick.

I entered the office and slammed the door behind me. My co-workers had never seen me like that before: I was shaking and visibly upset—they could tell something was wrong, and asked me what was going on. I couldn't even talk, all I could do was shake the phone, and tell them to watch the video.

It was a few minutes before I was able to settle down and tell them about the noise. They were impressed by the video, and needless to say none of us left the office for the rest of the night.

It wasn't too long that the video made the rounds of the office and everyone was talking about it, and speculating what it could be. I was the only one who wasn't participating in that. After the initial shock wore off, I was kind of embarrassed by the whole thing, as it was less than boss-like. I just wanted the whole thing to go away.

But of course, it didn't.

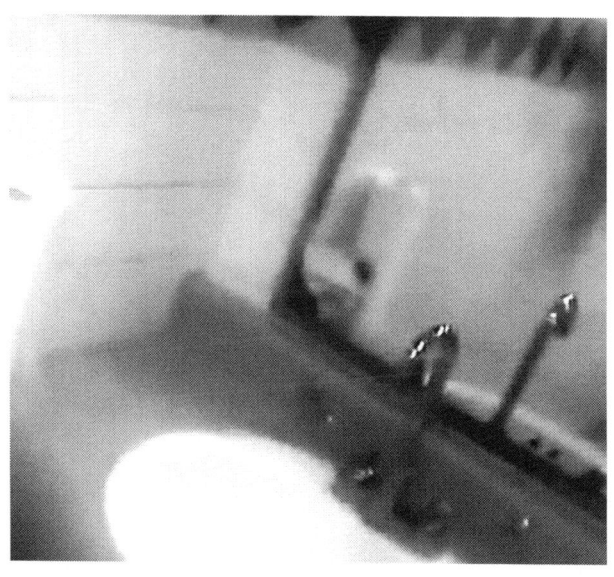

Bathroom scene from Eric's phone video: "...there was a crazy, windy, swooshing tornado-like noise..."

It was after this, that people starting talking about Tom again. Could it be Tom's spirit, or was it another of the thousands of people who have died in the building over the years?

Family and friends also watched the video; and one of my co-workers posted it on YouTube; someone said he watched it in slow motion and could hear all kinds of creepy things going on.

After that day, things got stranger around the office. There was something going on that we couldn't ignore anymore. There were all kinds of experiences:

- While walking down the hall, some said they would see themselves walking in the bubble mirrors that hang from the ceiling, but they'd also see someone walking behind them in the mirror. When they turned around nobody was there.
- My friend Becky felt her hair being tugged on.
- Joey heard strange voices while he was sitting in our office that were saying strange words like "sterile" and "breathe."
- One day the candy in the dispenser began rattling like there was a mouse in it or something, then it just fell over.
- Marcus went into the "haunted bathroom" and found the trashcan had been emptied out, and was sitting upside down on top of the toilet bowl.

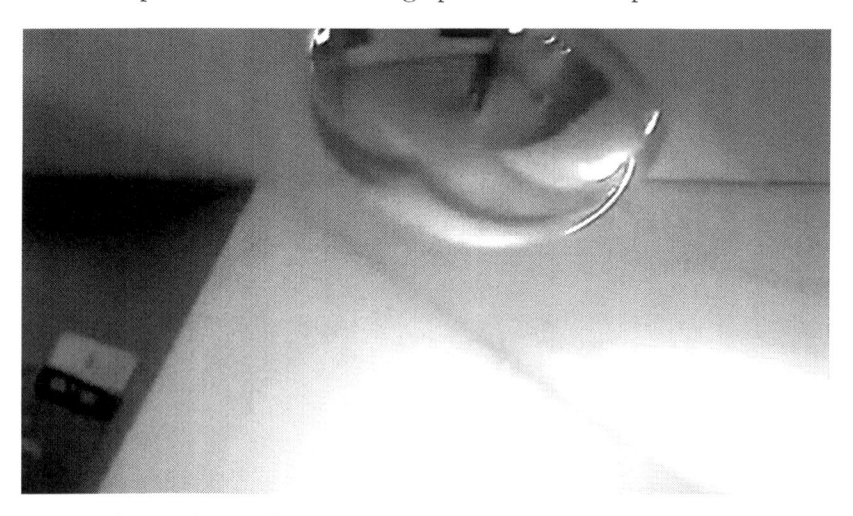

Hall mirror where employees said they would see someone walking behind them, but nobody was there. (Screenshot from Eric's phone video. That's Eric's reflection in the mirror, not a ghost).

So it began to appear that this wasn't a general haunting going on: it seemed like we were specifically being targeted for these experiences. And it was almost like there was a checklist; someone was making sure that every single person in the office experienced something they couldn't explain.

Some people didn't take it lightly, in fact Josie, the one who was chased in and out of the bathroom, ended up quitting—as did another rep. They said they just weren't comfortable working in that environment.

It had become so strange; it had become so spooky.

Things came to a head two-and-a-half weeks ago. It was a weeknight, and it was kind of a slow night. It was getting near the end of our shift when one my reps got a call from a doctor. The doctor said, "What's up with page you guys just sent me? It doesn't make any sense?"

So I got on the call and was trying to figure out what happened. I found out that he'd received a page that was complete gibberish: none of the words made sense. And while I was trying to deal with that, another doctor called another rep, and had a similar problem. He said, "I got this page, but it's identical to one I received two weeks ago."

So I started looking at that issue, and while I was doing that the phones started ringing and ringing and ringing…pretty soon all of our reps were on the phone with doctors from all over Salt Lake City, who received pages that didn't make any sense: some were gibberish; some were in foreign languages; some were regarding patients who had already died; some from pregnant patients who had already given birth months ago…the doctors were getting frustrated because they couldn't tell the difference between what was a real emergency, and what was a nonsense page.

So while my reps were dealing with the doctors' calls, I was on the phone with our IT department (waking them up and trying to figure out what was going on). Then I called the phone companies and the paging companies—everyone was blaming each other. Nobody seemed to know what was happening. But in the mean time, we had hundreds of doctors calling from the whole state wondering what was going on.

It all lasted about forty-five minutes, and then just as quickly as it started, it stopped.

One of our coworkers who has worked with our company for a long time, said she worked during the Troy Square Massacre, the Salt Lake City tornado, and during the Crandall Mine disaster—so she's been here for some crazy times, but she said nothing compared to what happened that night.

Our IT department spent days trying to figure out what happened, how it happened and how to keep it from happening again. But no explanation was ever found. To this day we don't know why those pages were going out. But it was chaos.

And that was when it finally hit me: this nonsense has gone on long enough. Like I said earlier, I'm a fixer: when there's a problem, I like to fix it. But I don't know what's going on here. We're losing good reps from my team—they're quitting because they don't like the environment. We could lose doctors who are not happy with our service. I could lose my job because this is all happening on my shift, and it makes me look incompetent...worse case scenario is someone could die because they aren't getting the service they need.

I'm a fixer. And I think the way to fix this, may be to share the story. And that's why I'm sharing this story—all this dirty laundry—because I want it to end. It's not fun—it's not funny anymore! Please, who ever is bothering us, we just want to be left alone. I don't know if it's Tom who is doing this. I don't know if he's listening. I don't know if he CAN listen. But if it is him, I make my confession, and I apologize to him for not letting him leave that afternoon he asked to leave.

I've lost so much sleep; I've spent so much thought wishing I could go back in time—wishing more than anything I could go back in time, and let him leave... tell him to leave—and don't go home...go straight to the emergency room and get yourself taken care of because there's something going on in your stomach—and it's going to go bad.

But I can't do that. What I can do is tell the story—make my confession; make my apology, and repent. I don't know if it will work or not. I don't know if I'll have more experiences like this to share. But I hope not...I hope this is the end of it.

Anything Ghost Show, Episode #170

Index of Names

Index of Public Domain Images

Page 104
"The Men in the Moon: or, the Devil to Pay"
Messrs Cobbett, Hunt
1820

Page 108
"New Operas, with Comical Stories, and Poems..."
D'Urfey, Thomas
1721

Page 113
"Death's Doings"
Dagley, Richard
1827

Page 121
"Illustrated Poems and Songs for Young People"
Barker, Lucy D. Sale
1885

Page 136
"Eene Halve Eeuw"
Ritter, Pierre Henri - the Elder
1898

18843767R00081

Made in the USA
Lexington, KY
24 November 2018